DISPUTED FRONTIERS

A PRELUDE TO CONFLICT ?

DISPUTED FRONTIERS

A PRELUDE TO CONFLICT ?

Reg Herschy

THE BOOK GUILD LTD
25 High Street
Lewes Sussex

This book is sold subject to the condition that it shall not, by way of trade or otherwise, be lent, re-sold, hired out, photocopied or held in any retrieval system or otherwise circulated without the publisher's prior consent in any form of binding or cover other than that in which this is published and without a similar condition including this condition being imposed on the subsequent purchaser.

The Book Guild Ltd.
25 High Street,
Lewes, Sussex

First published 1993
Copyright Reg Herschy 1993
Set in Times
Typesetting by Orbrad

Printed in Great Britain by
Antony Rowe Ltd.
Chippenham, Wiltshire.

A catalogue record for this book is available from the British Library

ISBN 0 86332 789

Dedicated to Lisl and our grandchildren

CONTENTS

	Introduction	
1	Disputed Frontiers of the Gulf	1
2	Palestine's Disputed Frontiers	13
3	The Berlin Wall	16
4	Transylvania's Disputed Frontiers	26
5	Czechoslovakia's Historic Frontiers	30
6	The Disputed Frontiers of Austria	34
7	The Attila Line	39
8	The Green Line	42
9	The Oder-Neisse Line	46
10	The Wilson, the Rapallo and the Morgan Lines	49
11	The 49th Parallel	59
12	The 17th Parallel	63
13	The 38th Parallel	66
14	The Radcliffe Line	71
15	The McMahon Line	78
16	The Curzon Line	80
17	China-Soviet Union Frontier Disputes	82
18	China-India Frontier Disputes	85
19	Japan-Soviet Union Islands Dispute	89
20	The Formosa Strait Disputed Frontier	91
21	The Disputed Territory of Antarctica	92
22	Gibraltar	95
23	Hong Kong	98
24	Northern Ireland	100
25	Africa's Disputed Frontiers	104
26	South America's Disputed Frontiers	110

27	Ethnic Frontiers under Dispute	117
28	Plebiscites as a Solution?	135
29	Epilogue	140
	Notes	142
	Bibliography	149
	Appendix : Frontier Decrees, 1918, 1941	157
	1. The Wilson Principles	157
	2. The Atlantic Charter	160
	Index	162

Maps:

The Treaty of Sèvres	2
The Middle East	4
The Changing frontiers of Israel	14
The Berlin Wall 1961-1989	18
The Treaty of Trianon	27
The Partitioning of Czechoslovakia	31
The fragmentation of Austria-Hungary	32
The Treaty of Versailles	33
The Treaty of St Germain-en-Laye	35
The Carinthian Question	36
The new states of Central Europe, 1920	38
Cyprus: The Attila (Green) Line	40
Beirut: The Green Line	43
The Oder-Neisse Line and Poland's postwar territorial adjustments	47

The Seven proposed lines to establish the Italy-Yugoslavia frontier, 1914-1954	55
The Oregan Boundary Dispute	60
Territorial growth of the United States	61
Disputed marine frontier between the United States and Canada	62
Vietnam: The 17th Parallel	64
Korea: The 38th Parallel	67
India-Pakistan frontier: 1947: The Ravi-Sutlej salient	73
The Radcliffe and McMahon Lines and the disputed frontiers of China-India, China-Commonwealth of Independent States. The 17th and 38th Parallels, Hong Kong, Formosa Strait and the disputed Senkaku Isles.	76/77
The Curzon Line (1921)	81
China-Commonwealth of Independent States frontiers	83
The Kurile Islands	89
Antarctica: Territorial claims	93
Gibraltar	96
Hong Kong	98
Northern Ireland	101
Africa's disputed frontiers	106
South America's disputed frontiers	112
Central America's disputed frontiers	115
The collapse of the Ottoman Empire	118
Serbia and its neighbours, 1878-1914	121
Yugoslavia, 1991	123
The Partition of Yugoslavia, 1941	124
The 15 republics of the former Soviet Union (now the Commonwealth of Independent States)	126

The Belgian Language Line	132
Plebiscites and Consultations held, attempted, or planned in Europe 1914-1939	137

ACKNOWLEDGEMENTS

Acknowledgement is gratefully made to the following for their permission to publish maps and photographs:

MAPS

Baedeker, London, Hong Kong, 1987; page 98

Carnegie Endowment for International Peace, Washington DC.
Plebiscites since the World War, Sarah Wambaugh, 1933; page 137
The Treaties of Peace, 1919-1923; pages 2, 27, 33, 35

Library of Congress, Federal Research Division, Washington DC
Poland: A Country Study, H.D. Nelson 1983; page 47
China: A Country Study, F.M. Bunge 1983; pages 76, 77, 83
Yugoslavia: A Country Study, R.F. Nyrop, 1982; page 124

George Weidenfeld and Nicolson, London,
First World War History Atlas, Martin Gilbert, 1970; pages 32, 38, 118, 121
Recent History Atlas 1800-1960, Martin Gilbert, 1977; pages 31, 112

Hamish Hamilton, London, The First Dance of Freedom, Martin Meredith, 1984; page 106

Harper Collins, New York, Encyclopedia of American History, Richard B. Norris, 1965; pages 60, 61

Hodder and Stoughton, London, An Atlas of Territorial and Border Disputes, David Downing, 1980; page 115

Hutchinson, London, The Making of Modern Lebanon, Helena Cobban, 1985; page 43

Informationzentrum, Berlin, 1985; page 18

Methuen, London, An Atlas of World Affairs, A. Boyd, 1987; pages 64, 67, 96, 101

National Geographic Society, Washington DC
    Antarctica, April 1987; page 93
    Common Ground Different Dreams, February 1990; page 62

Stavros Pantelli, A New History of Cyprus, 1984; page 40

Praeger GPG, New York, Austria, Karl Städler, 1971; page 36

Stryker-Post, Washington DC Western Europe, 1989; page 132

The Daily Telegraph,
    10 January 1991; page 4
    8 May 1991; page 123
    16 September 1991; page 89
    24 February 1992; page 73

The New York Times,
    13 March 1991; page 126
    29 October 1991; page 14

PHOTOGRAPHS

Plates are reproduced by kind permission of the Hulton Company, London and the Associated Press, London.

The photograph on the jacket is reproduced by kind permission of Cole/SIPA, New York.

INTRODUCTION

The world today is plagued by unresolved frontier disputes. Some have led to war and others, if not resolved, will remain potential flash points of conflict.

Many of today's frontiers were drawn within the last eighty years, some even more recently, and most have experienced stability. Europe's frontiers, some of which were drawn, or redrawn, at the Paris Peace Conference after the First World War, are in this category. Until the Berlin Wall was breached, these frontiers experienced stability for over forty years but age-old ethnic and religious grievances, suppressed under Nazism and Communism, have suddenly erupted into nationalistic claims for autonomy. While governments wrestle with these problems, xenophobia is rising and causing concern in some countries of central Europe.

The frontiers of the Gulf were arbitrarily drawn before oil was discovered, the frontiers of China and India were demarcated when China was weak, and all of these are now under dispute although they were acceptable by agreements or treaties at the time.

The hastily drawn frontiers between India and East and West Pakistan were completed in only five weeks and immediately led to 200,000 people being killed in communal and religious violence, leaving 12 million people homeless.

India and Pakistan have fought a war over Kashmir's disputed frontier, India and China have gone to war over their

Himalayan frontier, and China and the Soviet Union have clashed over their 4,000 miles frontier.

Until recently, the 17th Parallel separated North and South Vietnam and the Green Line separated East and West Beirut, but Korea is still divided at the 38th Parallel and the Attila Line still divides Cyprus.

Antarctica is owned by no-one but there are already outstanding territorial claims with various countries' proposed frontiers already mapped out. And although the 5,500 miles undefended United States-Canada 'friendly' frontier is almost free from dispute, fishing rights remain an issue on the west coast because of disagreement over the maritime border.

Historical agreement between countries on water rights can become a dangerous source of conflict and today 40 per cent of the world's population of 5000 million depends on water from a neighbouring country. Of the 200 or more rivers shared by two or more countries, several have already caused international conflict and the tension will increase as water needs increase.

The Kurds are determined to gain autonomy within their own frontiers and Belgium may split into two autonomous regions – Flanders and Wallonia. Even in the United Kingdom, the Scottish National Party wants Scotland to secede from the Union.

The Soviet Empire, haphazardly created by Stalin in the 1930s, has been torn apart with twenty of its twenty-three internal borders now under dispute. The downfall of Communism in the former Soviet Union may yet fuel internal border disputes in other Communist countries including China.

The Yugoslav Federation, stable for forty-five years, will collapse into civil war unless a formula can be found to satisfy its ethnic minorities and its internal borders redrawn. Serious disputes are arising in both South America and the African continent. In Asia, Japan and the Soviet Union (now the Commonwealth of Independent States) have still not signed a Second World War peace treaty because of a dispute over minor islands in the Pacific.

Four major wars have been fought between Israel and Arab

states over the frontiers of Israel and after each war new frontiers were established, all under dispute.

The Iron Curtain, a man-made frontier extending 2,500 miles from the Baltic to the Black Sea separating East from West was finally breached in 1989 after nearly forty years. The Berlin Wall, part of that frontier, had alone claimed the lives of eighty people, fifty-five of whom were shot down in cold blood by East German border guards while trying to escape.

South Tirol is still disputed by Austria, and Yugoslavia's claim on Southern Carinthia has never been renounced, although both claims are dormant. For the first time since the Paris Peace Treaty of 1920 which dismembered the Austro-Hungarian Empire, Hungarian newspapers in 1990 ran leading articles critical of the treaty which deprived Hungary of about half its territory and transferred one million Hungarians to Czechoslovakia, half a million to Yugoslavia and one and a half million to Romania.

After the Second World War, in spite of the Atlantic Charter (see appendix), territorial adjustments moved Poland's physical centre westwards and some 3 million people were removed from their homes in the eastern part of the country and resettled in the newly acquired western part from which 2.5 million Germans were in turn removed. Because of the Second World War and subsequent frontier changes, Poland's population fell from 35 million in 1939 to 25 million in 1950.

In this book 'frontier' and 'border' are used interchangeably although strictly the former may signify a zone whereas the latter usually denotes a line, often a watershed line or the thalweg line of a river. In many cases cited the frontier may be an ethnic one or even an enclave. Frontiers may be delimited as a result of war or conflict, by plebiscite, or even by territorial purchase as in the case of the British 99-year lease of the Hong Kong New Territories for the sum of £500 in 1898 or the United States purchase of Alaska in 1867 for about $7 million and the Gadsden Purchase of a strip of Mexican territory for $10 million in 1853.

As this book goes to press, frontiers in many parts of the world are still under dispute and are likely to be so for some time to come.

1

DISPUTED FRONTIERS OF THE GULF

The States and their Frontiers

The land and sea bed frontiers of the Persian Gulf states, once considered of little importance, took on significance when oil was discovered. Today the states between them supply some 40 per cent of the world's oil needs. During the second half of the 19th century, however, the economy of the Gulf states was in decline, but as British power there grew in the early part of the 20th century, a sense of stability led to great improvements. The British generally delegated responsibility to the East India Company and later to the Governments of Bombay and India. From the end of the Second World War until the United Arab Emirates (UAE) became independent, the British Foreign Office handled all Gulf matters through political agents in Bahrain, Qatar, Abu Dhabi and Dubai. Under various treaties, however, these states never actually came under British sovereignty but all external affairs were handled by Britain and military forces were stationed in Oman, Sharjah and Bahrain.[1]

By the 1960s, however, Britain began granting full independence to the Gulf states. Kuwait was first in 1961 and Bahrain, Qatar and the UAE followed in 1971.

Until then Britain had maintained peace and stability in the Gulf and British officials had arbitrated in local disputes, but after the withdrawal of the British forces and civil and public servants, old territorial claims and suppressed tribal animosities came to the surface again.

The present Middle East frontiers were drawn by the Western Allies during the Paris Peace Conference between 1918 and

1923. The Ottoman (Turkish) Empire, on the side of the Central Powers during the First World War, was dissolved by the Treaties of Sèvres (1920), Lausanne (1923) and the Sykes-Picot Agreement (1916).[2] The territory of the Empire was settled between the new Gulf states but the frontiers are still undefined and in most cases under dispute.

In the case of Oman, for example, the frontiers remain unfixed and the size of the country is therefore unknown. The Government of Oman uses an estimate of 120,000 square miles, but most observers suggest an area of only 85,000 square miles.

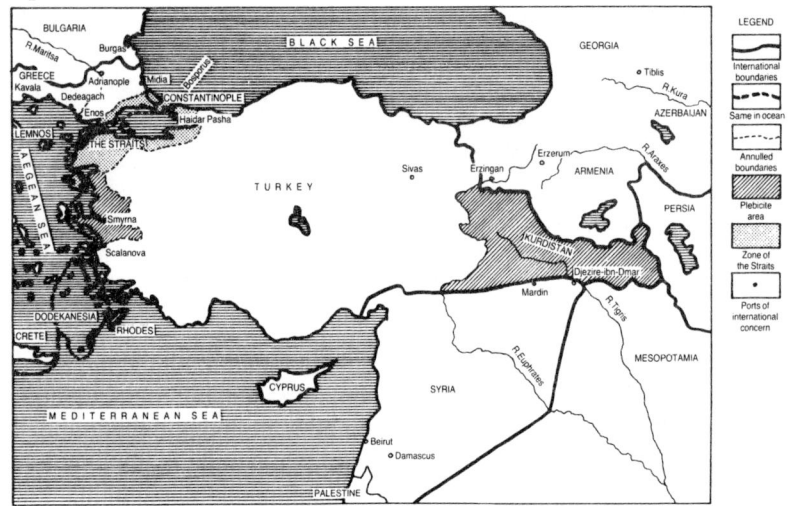

The Treaty of Sèvres

Whilst the definition of some of the frontiers, such as the delineation of the Syrian-Iraqi frontier, presented little difficulty at the time, others have caused considerable unrest. The frontier between Syria and Palestine depended to a large extent on the available water supply to Palestine. Britain was the mandatory power in both Palestine and Iraq while France had mandatory powers over the Lebanon and Syria. The British maintained that the successful economic development of Palestine depended on water supply both for power and irrigation and that there was not sufficient water resources for these purposes within the designated frontiers. Water existed only in rivers flowing through the border districts between Syria and Palestine – in the Litani River, the upper Jordan, and the Yarmuk River, itself a tributary of the Jordan. But these rivers lay within the Syrian region provisionally assigned to France by the Sykes-Picot Agreement. France at first refused to make concessions but finally agreed to grant Palestine the privilege of using, within French territory, the surplus waters of the upper Jordan and the Yarmuk, but not of the Litani, and the frontier was provisionally settled accordingly.

Today Israel draws its water from three main sources – the western coastal aquifer, the eastern heights aquifer, and 25 per cent from the Sea of Galilee (Lake Kenneret) – but still has a severe water problem. Water is scarce in the whole region and the future of shared water in the Middle East will remain in the forefront of any peace negotiations. Indeed, if there is another war over frontiers in the Middle East it will be over the control of the scarce water resources and not over abundant oil.[3]

The dominant powers of the Gulf are Saudi Arabia, Iraq and Iran, the smaller states being Kuwait, Bahrain, Qatar, the UAE and Oman. These small states have been intimidated over the years by their more powerful neighbours. Iran has laid claim to Bahrain, Iraq to Kuwait and Saudi Arabia to selected parts of the UAE.

Territorial claims

The Iranian claim to Bahrain is based on their 17th century occupation of that state after the Iranian defeat of Portugal. Iran was later forced out of Bahrain by the present ruling family, the Al Khalifa. In a United Nations plebiscite in 1971, the people of Bahrain declared their independence and the Shah of Iran instead occupied the Gulf islands of Abu Musa and the Turbs. There was no outcry from the West

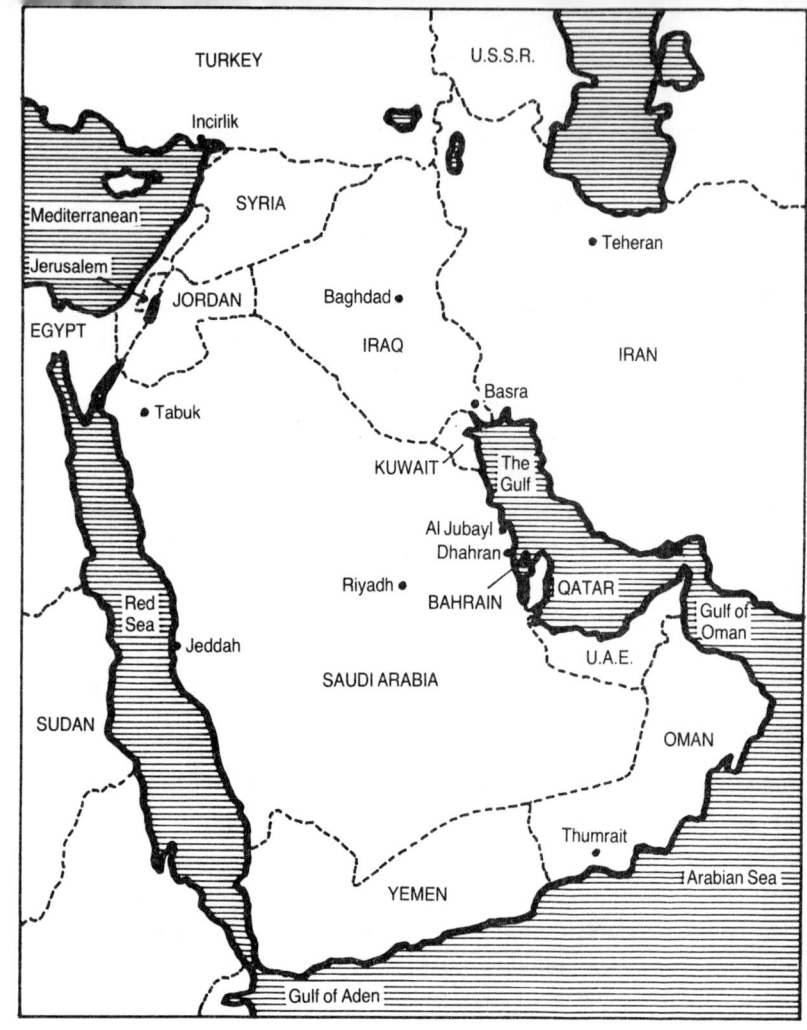

The Middle East

over the occupation of the islands because the Shah was a friend and ally and the affair was written off as a local dispute that should not concern the West. The occupation is now considered a *fait accompli* but the islands are still under claim by Sharjah and Ras al Khaymah respectively, and it was because of their occupation that Iraq broke off diplomatic relations with Iran. However, when the Ayatollah replaced the Shah, the Iranian claim to Bahrain was revived. To add confusion to the issue, Bahrain still lays claim to the Hawar Islands and Az Zabarah on the Qatar coast. This claim is based upon the Bahrain contention that the Al Khalifa settled at Az Zabarah in the 18th century before driving the Iranians out of Bahrain. But for this claim the seven entities that became the UAE in 1971 might have been nine if Qatar and Bahrain had settled their disputed frontiers.

Another local border dispute concerns the inlet Khawr al Udayd at Abu Dhabi which had been placed under sovereignty of that state by the British. The British ruling, however, was contested by Qatar and Saudi Arabia, both of whom laid claim to the inlet. The dispute was further complicated by a disagreement over the Buraymi Oasis in the UAE in which Abu Dhabi, Oman, and Saudi Arabia had all been involved since as long ago as 1969. The dispute was settled in 1974 by an ambiguous agreement on a new frontier between the UAE and Saudi Arabia. The UAE was given six villages in the oasis and Oman three; Saudi Arabia secured a corridor to the Gulf through UAE territory. However, the three states have yet to publish definitive frontiers and the oasis meantime continues to be occupied peacefully by the tribes of all three states.

The Oman enclave on the tip of the Musandam Peninsula which provides a shoreline for Oman on the Gulf has achieved international importance because of its position on the Strait of Hormuz. This territory has been claimed by the UAE and the frontier was under dispute just prior to the Iran-Iraq War. Within a year of the Iraq invasion of Iran in 1980, the Gulf states of Saudi Arabia, Kuwait, Bahrain, Qatar, the UAE and Oman established the Gulf Cooperation Council (GCC) to strengthen economic and cultural ties among the states.[4]

The Shatt al Arab Waterway

The 120 miles long Shatt al Arab Waterway, into which the rivers Tigris and Euphrates empty at the town of Al Qurnah (the supposed site of the Garden of Eden), has been the subject of a long-standing frontier dispute between Iran and Iraq. Although the causes of the eight year war between these states were deeply embedded in religion, nationalism and economics, the possession of the Shatt al Arab Waterway was an important Iraqi objective and was used as an excuse to invade Iran. The dispute over the sovereignty of the waterway, which forms the Iraq-Iran frontier, dates back some 400 years or more and has featured in at least twenty-five wars. The waterway is of vital importance to Iraq because it has only 10 miles of Gulf coast to Iran's 1400 miles.[5]

Although Iraq's relations with other neighbours were generally cordial during the mid-seventies, despite unresolved disputes over frontiers with Kuwait, the complicated three-cornered Iraq, Turkey, and Syria arrangement of sharing the waters of the Euphrates and Tigris ever remained a potential danger. These rivers which rise in Turkey are essential to the life of these countries, but they may also threaten it.[6] Iraq's present frontiers are not based on natural features but on the results of wars and diplomacy. The State of Iraq was a Class A Mandate of Britain until independence in 1932, a status conferred upon it by the Allies after the First World War under the Treaties of Sèvres and Iraq (1922). The new frontiers, however, were drawn with little correspondence to the physical location of ethnic and religious groups, and the definition of these borders has played a large part in Iraq's problems during the last 70 years.

Disputes with Iran over navigation rights resulted in the Frontier Treaty (1937), a treaty negotiated between the two states under British auspices. This treaty established that the international frontier would, in part, be at the low water mark on the Iranian side of the Shatt al Arab waterway. This provision, however, became a source of contention between the two states. Iran insisted that the 1937 treaty had been imposed on it by 'British imperialist pressures', that it was a violation of common international practice and that the proper frontier was the thalweg of the channel based on the depth of water. The issue came to a head in 1969 when Iraq told Iran that the waterway might be closed to Iranian navigation and that the Shatt al Arab was an integral part of Iraqi territory. Iranian gunboats were immediately sent down the waterway but met no Iraqi resistance. However, by a border treaty in 1975, signed by the Shah for Iran and the then Foreign Minister Saddam Hussein for Iraq, the waterway frontier was defined along the thalweg and the land frontier defined according to the maps drawn for the 1914 border agreement.

In 1979 the Shah of Iran was deposed and in the same year Saddam Hussein became President of Iraq and promptly tore up the 1975 treaty. After ten months of intermittent skirmishing over the sovereignty of the waterway, Iraq and Iran embarked on a war which lasted eight years (1980-8) and claimed one million casualties. After the war, although Iraq controlled the Shatt al Arab Waterway, Saddam Hussein decided to settle the long-standing dispute and the frontier returned to the thalweg of the waterway.[7]

Kuwait's disputed frontiers

As recently as 1940, Kuwait City was only a small insignificant walled town of mud huts, but its growth after the Second World War was rapid and today it is a modern metropolis with a skyscraper business centre and villa-style suburbs. Oil had been discovered in 1938 but was not exploited until after the war. Many Gulf states have modelled their social welfare on Kuwait's success. The frontiers of Kuwait are shared with Saudi Arabia in the south and Iraq in the north. The area of the state is about 7,000 square miles including a number of offshore islands, the largest of which is Bubiyan separated from the mainland by a narrow waterway.

The original frontier with Iraq dates from a 1913 agreement between Kuwait, represented by British officials, and the Ottoman Empire. Although never finally ratified, this agreement was accepted by Iraq in 1932 when Iraq became independent. However, when Britain decided to terminate its protectorate of Kuwait in 1961 and recognise Kuwait's independence, Iraq took immediate advantage of the situation and laid claim to Kuwait territory which Iraq maintained was once part of the province of Al Basrah in the Ottoman Empire.

The frontier between Kuwait and Saudi Arabia was agreed by the 1922 Treaty of Uqair which also defined the Kuwait and Saudi Arabia neutral zone, an area of some 800 square miles. Kuwait's security has always centred on its relations with its three large neighbours – Iraq, Iran and Saudi Arabia – and during the Iraq-Iran War, which raged only 50 miles from its northern frontier, Kuwait got caught in the crossfire.

Although Kuwait was initially neutral in the conflict, in 1981 it began supporting Iraq with loans totalling $6 billion over a two year period and allowing Iraq-bound trade to enter Kuwait ports and cross its northern frontier. However, in October 1981 Iranian jets attacked Kuwait's oil facilities at Umm al Aysh as a warning against Kuwait's support of Iraq and it is believed that the 1983 terrorist bombing in Kuwait City was another Iranian warning to cease support of Iraq. In fact Kuwait feared the victory of either side because each of the antagonists was considered a potential enemy, but Iraq was perhaps thought the lesser of two evils at the time.

Iraq's 1961 claim to the whole territory of Kuwait was somewhat eased two years later when a new government in Iraq finally recognised the independence of Kuwait. However, this agreement did not apparently involve an acceptance of Kuwait's frontier and fighting broke out between the two states on 20 March 1973 when, in the view of most foreign observers Iraq attacked a Kuwaiti border post overlooking Umm Qasr and the nearby islands of Al Warbah and Bubiyan in the Gulf. Iraqi troops abandoned the border post sixteen days later under international pressure.

During the next few years, tension remained high and several Iraqi incursions into Kuwait's disputed border territory were reported until eventually a joint ministerial committee was set up to help resolve the dispute and relations began to improve. Iraq has persistently maintained that Kuwait was wholly a creation of British imperialism whose frontiers were drawn up by Britain in 1923. In fact Kuwait had been an autonomous sheikdom under the al-Sabah family since 1756 and had a treaty of protection with Britain from 1899 until independence in 1961.[8]

It can be argued that Turkey had a stronger case for claiming the return of the Mosul than Iraq had for annexing Kuwait, since the former Ottoman province, including the Kurdish city of Kirkuk, was awarded by Britain to the new state of Iraq under the Treaties of Lausanne and Iraq. After the outbreak of the Iraq-Iran war, Iraq again pressed its claim for the cession of the islands of Al Warbah and Bubiyan since its port of Basra was closed. Kuwait, in again rejecting the claim, responded by building a causeway from the mainland to Bubiyan in order to secure its position on the island.

As the war continued Kuwait feared an escalation involving not only the Gulf states but also the two super-powers and endeavoured to initiate a negotiated peace through the GCC by which the aid to Iraq was channelled. Nothing came of this attempt to stop the war and Iraq continued to have designs on Kuwaiti territory.

The war eventually ended in a virtual stalemate and a strained form of peace reigned in the Gulf until 1990 when, to the surprise of the world, at 2 am on 2 August Saddam Hussein's vast army, with an available strength of one million men and 4,000 tanks, invaded Kuwait and Kuwait became the 19th province of Iraq.

The decision to compel Iraq to quit Kuwait was near-unanimous in the Arab world and beyond, and supported by no less than twelve United Nations Security Council resolutions. The vote of the five permanent members – Britain, France, China, USA, and USSR was unanimous for the first time under such circumstances, and under Resolution 678 of 29 November 1990, a deadline was set for Iraq to evacuate Kuwait by midnight US Eastern Standard Time (5 am GMT) on 15 January 1991. Thereafter the twenty-eight-nation coalition, led by the US, was authorised to use force if necessary. Iraq refused to retreat and the deadline came and went. Just before midnight GMT, on 17 January, Allied Operation Desert Storm was launched with 1,300 combat jets and 1,500 attack helicopters. Five weeks later at precisely 1 am on 24 February the Allies launched a massive ground invasion of Kuwait and in the space of only 100 hours, the country was liberated. Iraq had lost 45 per cent of her tanks, 40 per cent of her artillery and 50 per cent of her aircraft. The battle was over but the disputed frontiers of the Gulf remained unresolved. A Demilitarized Zone (DMZ) between Iraq and Kuwait was established some 15 miles deep and 120 miles long.

The frontiers of 'Greater Kurdistan'

For over seventy years the most important persistent security threat to Iraq and other Middle East states has been the resistance of the strong, almost fanatical, Kurdish minority. The restless Iraqi Kurds live mostly in an area around Mosul in the north of Iraq and, before the Gulf War, virtually controlled some 250 miles of mountainous terrain along the Iraqi-Turkish-Iranian frontiers. The Kurds have occupied their territory for three thousand years, have a common language and culture, and are a nation in all but statehood.

The Kurdish rebellion erupted in 1919 in a ferocious campaign against the authority of the British Mandate of Iraq in an effort to establish a Kurdish state. Their struggle against the Iraqi government has gained strength in an effort to attain either autonomy within Iraq or complete independence outside Iraq. After another rebellion in 1925-6 the League of Nations decided that the British Mandate conditions in the Anglo-Iraq Treaty of 1922 be extended from four years to twenty-five years to protect the country from Turkish claims on the Mosul province with its vast oil resources.

The Kurdish minority in Mosul hated the Arabs and the large numbers of fiercely independent armed Kurds in Iraqi territory has continued to be a serious problem for the government. During the Ottoman Empire the Kurds reluctantly supported the Ottomans in exchange for a measure of autonomy and remained substantially loyal to them during the First World War.

After the war, in accordance with the Treaty of Sèvres, the Allies tentatively agreed to a separate Kurdish state to be known as 'Greater Kurdistan' and the proposed frontier would have generally surrounded an area bordered by Iraq

(Mesopotamia), Turkey, Iran (Persia) and Syria, but the anti-Kurd Ataturk regime resisted the proposal and the plan was dropped. It is estimated that such an autonomous state today would have a population of some twenty million people, made up of Kurd enclaves in Iraq, Syria, Iran, Turkey and the Soviet Union (now the CIS).

During the last decade Iraq has consistently underestimated the Kurdish desire for autonomy and certainly showed little sympathy towards the creation of a 'Kurdistan'. Each spring and summer the central government won territory from the Kurds only to lose it again in the autumn. The Iraqis have used air power, rockets, tanks and napalm during incursions into Kurdish 'territory', but the Kurds are masters of guerilla tactics, and in December 1963 they actually advanced as far south as Khanaqin, about 100 miles from Baghdad. A cease-fire was agreed only in February 1964 and the government assured the Kurds that their national claims for a measure of independence or autonomy would be recognised in a new constitution and an amnesty would be declared.

The Kurds were cautious enough to retain their arms until the constitution was firmly established because negotiations broke down and hostilities resumed again, casualties being heavy on both sides. Skirmishes overflowed across the Iran-Iraq frontier and the violation of Iran's frontiers made an already tense relation between the two countries even worse.

In 1966, in order to improve a situation which was fast becoming insoluble, Iraq agreed to formulate proposals towards a settlement in which, as a first step, the Kurdish language would have a status equal to Arabic, and health and education would be independently administered. In return Iraq called for the 15,000 strong Kurdish armed forces to be disbanded, but hostilities broke out again lasting from 1968 to 1969. The success of the Kurds in these conflicts was blamed by Iraq on the aid which the Kurds received from Iran and Israel.

By 1970 little had been resolved, but in that year a further effort was made in a fifteen article peace plan in which it was proposed that the Kurds would have five cabinet appointments in the government and could retain their army which would become an official Iraqi frontier force to be known as the Pesh Merga ('those who face death'). This plan was apparently unsatisfactory because the delineation of what was in fact Kurdish territory remained unresolved and at the time of signing the peace plan the Kurds claimed control of territory from Zakhu in the north to Halabjah in the south, and already imposed Kurdish administration in most of the towns in that area.[9]

The Kurdish Democratic Party (KDP) was granted official recognition as the legitimate representative of the Kurdish people but the Kurdish Workers Party (PKK) was also a strong separatist movement both in Iraq and Turkey. Indeed South East Turkey has been under virtual martial law for most of the past 10 years since the PKK started a terror campaign. Their cat-and-mouse tactics with the Turkish army in the rugged mountainous terrain of Cudi has often tied down more than 60,000 Turkish troops and estimates reveal that thousands have been killed on both sides. According to Amnesty International the Turkish authorities have imprisoned and tortured thousands of Kurds. During and after the cease-fire of the Iraqi-Iranian war in 1988, Iraq attacked the rebellious Kurds in the mountains with bombs and chemical weapons causing enormous casualties and forcing mass migration across the frontier to Turkey.

After the Gulf War, the Kurds saw an opportunity to rebel against Iraqi rule and soon occupied all territory as far south as Kirkuk and controlled that town for six days in March 1991 until they were ruthlessly driven out by the Iraqi army's counter-offensive spearheaded by tanks, artillery and helicopter gunships. Over the next few days the retreat of the Kurds was complete, and as many as two million refugees fled to the mountains and escaped to Turkey or Iran. Over 70 per cent of this ragged trail of humanity were women and children, and hundreds died by the roadside or in the snow-clad mountains. In April, however, the Allies established a safe zone or 'enclave' in Iraq, north of the 36th Parallel, to where the Kurds could return pending talks with the Iraqi leadership.[10]

2

PALESTINE'S DISPUTED FRONTIERS

The Arab-Israeli conflict has dominated Middle East politics since 1948. Four major wars have been fought between the Arab states and Israel since then with substantial casualties, and the conflict has even spilled into Lebanon.

After each war a variety of new frontiers was established, all of them leading to further disputes. Since its inception on 14 May 1948, when the British withdrew and the state of Israel was proclaimed on the same day, Israel has expanded beyond its 1948 frontiers into the West Bank and Gaza (1967), Sinai (1956, 1967, 1973), the Golan Heights (1967, incorporated officially in 1981). In 1978 it also established a buffer zone in South Lebanon. Israel has justified this expansion and the large numbers of settlements on the occupied West Bank on the grounds that it needed to secure its frontiers to protect its people from incursions and guerilla attacks.

Palestine, with a Jewish minority, was ruled from the 11th century as a part of non-Arab empires, the last of these being the Ottoman Empire which, with the exception of the Crusader interval from 1098 to 1291, ruled for four centuries. The country was taken by Britain in 1917 during the First World War. Britain pledged to support a Jewish national homeland there, as foreseen by the Zionists. In 1920 a British-Palestine Mandate was established and frontiers agreed, and in 1922 the land east of the River Jordan was detached.[1]

The Arabs rejected partition and, immediately after the British withdrawal, the Arab states of Egypt, Jordan, Syria, Lebanon, Iraq and Saudi Arabia invaded Israel but failed to destroy the Jewish state and were defeated. The greater part of Palestine

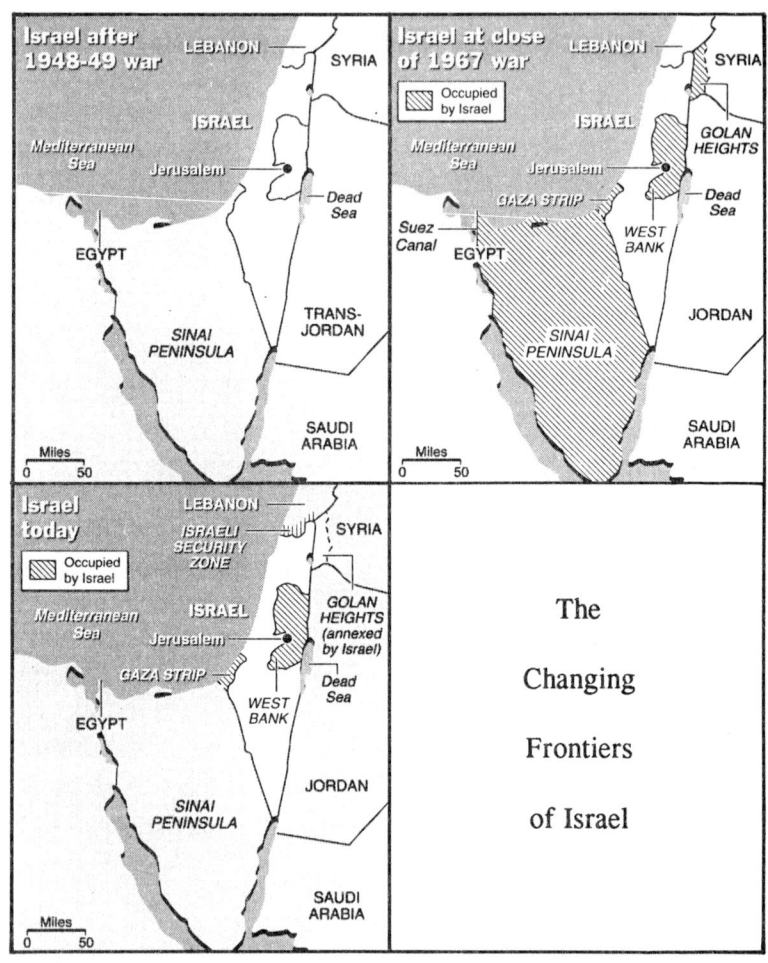

The Changing Frontiers of Israel

became the Jewish state of Israel. Most of the rest was amalgamated with Transjordan to become Jordan, and the Gaza Strip was occupied by Egypt. Two thirds of the Palestinian Arabs became refugees in Jordan, Gaza, Syria and Lebanon. After the 1948 war, the refugees wished to return to their homes and the Palestinians in general wanted to have their own state. Israel refused to accept their claims and the Arab states in turn refused to recognise Israel. The disagreement states in turn refused to recognise Israel. The disagreement led to three further wars: Suez, 29 October - 6 November 1956; The Six Day War, 5-10 June 1967; Yom Kippur, 6-24 October 1973.[2]

In The Six Day War, Israel pushed out its existing frontiers and took the Gaza Strip and the Sinai Peninsula; it captured Old Jerusalem, Syria's Golan Heights and Jordan's West Bank. In the Yom Kippur War, Israel pushed its frontier across the Suez Canal. After the Yom Kippur War, Israel agreed, in 1974, to withdraw from the Suez Canal's West Bank, and in a second withdrawal in 1976 agreed to move the frontier east to a line from El Arish on the Mediterranean to Ras Muhammed on the Red Sea. Finally, in 1982, Israel agreed to withdraw completely from the Sinai Peninsula to a new frontier on a line from Rafah, on the Mediterranean, to Aqaba.

In 1978 Israel invaded southern Lebanon to counter guerilla attacks by the Palestinian Liberation Organisation (PLO), and, in 1982, advanced as far as Beirut, opening a new frontier of Arab-Israeli tension. In October 1987 resistance to Israeli rule began to gather momentum in the West Bank and Gaza, and a year later some 300 Palestinian civilians were killed by Israeli troops.

Since the Gulf War, The United States has made several efforts at conferences on Middle East disputes, including the Arab-Israeli issue, but, so far, all have ended in failure.

3

THE BERLIN WALL

Early on a cold November morning in 1989 Europe's notorious frontier, the Berlin Wall, was finally breached and the people of East Berlin surged into the West with spontaneous tears of joy. A man-made frontier which had separated East and West Berlin for twenty-eight years and claimed some eighty lives had suddenly collapsed. The incredible news was broadcast to East Berlin by television on Thursday night, the 9 November. The gate was open they were told, they were free to go. The Wall had enslaved East Berliners and a country of 17 million people. Not only had a frontier crumbled but a whole ideology had vanished.

The Wall is built

The Wall was built because of the imposition of the Communist regime on the people in the Soviet Zone of Germany (the German Democratic Republic or GDR). Between 1949 and 1961 some 2.6 million people left East Germany for the West and half of these used Berlin as an escape route. By 1961 this had turned into a tidal wave. In July alone of that year some 30,000 refugees escaped to the West. Under increasing pressure to stop this mass flight of people from East Germany, the leaders in Moscow and East Berlin decided to shift from the offensive to the defensive to solve the Berlin problem. At the same time the following decree of the GDR Council of Ministers was declared.[1]

> To put an end to the hostile activities and militarise forces of Western Germany and West Berlin, control is to be introduced on the borders of the German

Democratic Republic, including the border with the Western sectors of Greater Berlin, which is usually introduced along the borders of every sovereign state. Reliable safeguards and effective control must be insured on the West Berlin borders in order to block the way to the subversive activities. The citizens of the German Democratic Republic may cross these borders only with special permission.

In the early morning of 13 August 1961, 60,000 commuters from East Berlin and East Germany were cut off from their work places in West Berlin. First the pavement was torn up at eighty sector border street crossings, then concrete posts were rammed into the ground and linked by barbed wire entanglements and deep defensive trenches dug along the line of the border. Underground and metropolitan railway traffic between the sectors was interrupted, but not until several days later did the GDR start building the Wall proper out of concrete slabs and hollow concrete blocks. Doorways and entrance gates to graveyards located directly at the sector border were sealed off by brick walls, and for the time being fourteen crossing-points between the two halves of the city remained open.

On 23 August the GDR set up offices at metropolitan railway stations to issue passes for visits to East Berlin, thus laying claim to sovereign rights in the Western Sectors. At the order of the Allied Kommandatura the West Berlin Police closed the offices three days later. From this time on, the GDR refused to admit the inhabitants of the Western Sector into the Eastern Sector.

The Wall extended 30 miles through Berlin, dividing the two parts of the city from each other, and 75 miles around the Western Sectors of the city, separating West Berlin from the GDR. Behind the Wall of concrete slabs and metal railings there was an illuminated strip of no-man's-land marked off by a trench with iron posts to prevent vehicles from breaking through. This was followed by a road for patrolling border guards, watch-towers, shelters and a network of watch-dogs chained to posts by long leashes, each one guarding his sector of the border on both sides of the chain-post. A 'contact' fence that released sound and light signals when touched completed the fortifications. The Berlin Wall completed an already fortified frontier, erected as early as 1952, extending 2,500 miles from the Baltic to the Black Sea.[2]

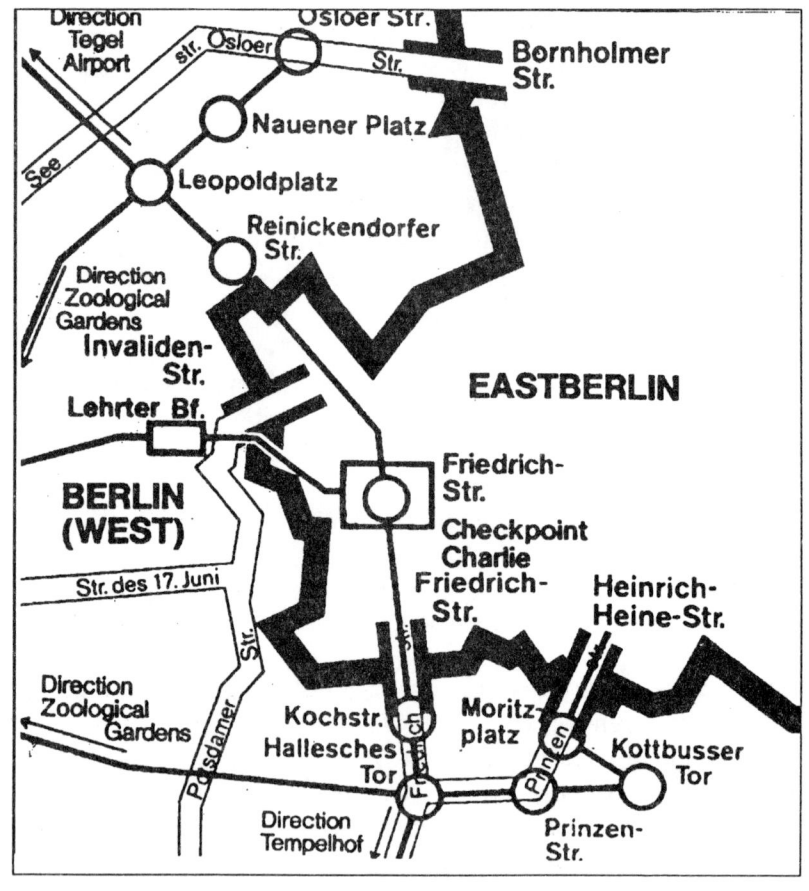

The Berlin Wall 1961-1989

Escape from East Berlin

In the 28 years of the wall, fifty-five of the eighty people who lost their lives trying to escape were shot down by GDR border guards and 112 people were wounded by gunshots. Just under 39,000 people, of whom over 500 were members of the 'Armed Forces' of the GDR, managed to escape to the Western part of the city before the Wall came down. From West Berlin over 3,000 people were observed being arrested while trying to escape. The number of attempted escapes that failed cannot be ascertained, but despite the fact that the GDR continuously perfected its frontier fortifications about 120 people escaped annually from East Berlin and the GDR to West Berlin. On 13 August 1981, the 20th anniversary of the erection of the Wall, Erich Honecker called the event 'a great contribution to safeguarding peace,'[3] but US President Ronald Reagan declared:[4]

> The Berlin Wall is a dramatic example of the desperate and cruel extremes to which totalitarian regimes will go to deny their subjects contact with other Europeans.

On this same day West Berlin's Governing Mayor Richard von Weizsacher called the Wall 'a petrified rejection of humanity.'[5]

Checkpoint Charlie

There were twenty-four crossing points into East Berlin. One of the most renowned was the Gleinicke Bridge which linked Potsdam with West Berlin and was the setting for East-West spy swaps.[6] Another was Checkpoint Charlie, a symbol of Berlin and the Cold War where Soviet and US tanks faced each other in October 1961. Checkpoint Charlie was the scene of many tragic escape attempts and was the only gate open to the Western Allies, non-Germans and tourists, who were permitted to stay on a one-day pass in East Berlin until midnight. The Iron Curtain had become impregnable.

Potsdam Conference

To try and understand this extraordinary episode in European history we have to return to 1945 to the conference of the wartime allies held in the beautiful Palace of Sanssouci in Potsdam just outside Berlin. At this conference the unity of Germany and Berlin's role as its capital city were not called into question. Germany would return to its 1937 frontiers but with four zones of occupation. The Soviet zone surrounded Berlin and an Allied Kommandatura came into effect immediately after the war for the administration of the city. A similar situation existed in Austria with its capital, Vienna, until 1955.

Berlin Blockade

However, in 1948, the Soviet representative withdrew from the Allied Kommandatura and later the Soviets declared that they would no longer participate in its meetings. The Soviet Union was determined that Germany should be divided so that it could cause no future threat to the East. In order to gain control over the whole of Berlin, or at least to delay the integration of West Berlin into West Germany, the Soviets launched the Berlin Blockade on 24 June 1948 when all frontier crossings via road, rail or waterway into Berlin were closed.

So critical was the situation that Allied military leave in both Germany and Austria was cancelled and demobilisation frozen. To counteract these closures and to maintain supplies into West Berlin, the Western Allies launched the Berlin Airlift. The air lift began on 26 June when the Western Allies flew 120 tons of goods into the city. Within a few weeks, however, the daily capacity of the air lift increased to about 4,000 tons. To accommodate this, Tegel Airport was built in the record time of 3 months, and eight other airfields in West Germany were placed at the disposal of the air lift. In April 1949, some 12,940 tons of goods were flown into West Berlin in a single day, the cargo planes landing at two minute intervals. The air lift was a feat unparalleled in the history of air transport and not only guaranteed the food supply for the population but maintained the economy of West Berlin.

By the winter of 1948-9 the Soviet Union realised that its manoeuvre to conquer the city was doomed and the eleven months blockade was finally lifted on 12 May 1949, and the last plane landed at Tempelhof on 30 September. In the course of the air lift, the military aircraft of the three Western Allies transported nearly two million tons of goods in more than 277,000 flights. Seventy members of the Allied air forces and eight German members of the ground personnel lost their lives in accidents. The memorial at Tempelhof Airport was erected in their memory.[7]

A frontier is imposed

After the Blockade the three Western Occupation Powers became Protection Powers. The East mark was no longer accepted as legal tender in the Western Sector and on 7 October 1949 the GDR was proclaimed in East Berlin and a frontier was imposed between the Germanies which would survive for forty years. Ernst Reuter, later Mayor of West Berlin declared in a protest rally before the Reichstag (Parliament):[8]

> People of the World! People of America, England, France and Italy! Look at the City and see that you cannot, must not abandon it and its people.

On 27 May, 1952, the German Democratic Republic suspended the telephone connections between the two halves of Berlin and, after increasing obstruction of inter-city bus and tramway traffic, restricted individual travel into the Soviet Zone. Travellers had to apply for residence permits at the People's Police stations in the Eastern Sector of the city. In July 1952 Berliners residing in the Western Sectors who owned homes or real estate in the Soviet Zone were denied access to their property. And finally, on 15 January 1953, tramway and bus lines running through both parts of the city were broken off.

The Workers' Strike
On 15 and 16 June 1953, three months after Stalin's death, a strike by East Berlin construction workers developed into a popular uprising against the Communist regime. On 17 June, at meetings held in all large factories in the Eastern Sector, the workers' demands, that work norms which had just been raised, be lowered again, escalated into other political areas, resulting in a demand for the government to resign and hold free elections. The demonstrations, which also spread to numerous cities in the Soviet Zone, resulted in violence, and at noon on 17 June the Soviet Military Commandant of the Soviet Sector declared a state of martial law. Soviet tanks intervened and put down the uprising. The exact number of dead and wounded has never been disclosed. People involved in this first uprising within the Communist sphere of influence learned from experience that aid and direct intervention from the West were impossible.

Berlin Conference
The Council of Foreign Ministers held its Berlin Conference from 25 January to 18 February 1954, in both halves of the city. At this meeting the Soviet Union rejected a proposal by the British Foreign Minister, Anthony Eden, to reunify Germany. Following the conference the three Western Powers made a guarantee declaration for Berlin and announced that they[9]

> Will do everything in their power to improve the situation in Berlin and promote the economic welfare of the city.

The Cold War
'Bastion of freedom', 'showcase of the West,' 'thorn in the flesh of the GDR' are some of the catch-phrases which were coined during the Cold War to describe the function of the free part of Berlin. The city was a refuge for many people who had left the Communist sphere of influence for political

reasons or felt attracted by the economic prosperity and cultural variety of the West. The continuous drain on the East German labour force aggravated the GDR's economic and political problems, which in turn affected the whole Communist power structure in Eastern Europe. Measures the GDR felt it had to resort to, such as enacting a passport law on 19 December 1957, to stiffen the penalty for 'fleeing the Republic' and imposing even more severe sanctions against people they caught visiting the Western Sectors without authorization, were not conducive to stabilising the situation.

The Soviet Prime Minister Nikita Khrushchev tried to solve this problem in his own way. On 10 November 1958, he emphasized in a speech in Moscow:[10]

> Apparently the time has come that the signatory powers of the Potsdam Agreement should relinquish the occupation regime in Berlin in order to normalize the situation in the Capital of the German Democratic Republic. The Soviet Union on its part will transfer to the sovereign GDR those functions in Berlin which are still performed by the Soviet authorities.

In a note to the Western Powers on 27 November, the Soviet Government demanded the withdrawal of Western troops and 'the conversion of West Berlin into an independent political unit - a free city'. In case the Western Powers should not be willing to negotiate on these demands, the Soviet Union threatened to 'carry out the planned measures through an agreement with the GDR', according to which the GDR would 'exercise its sovereignty on land, on water, and in the air' and hence terminate Allied rights in the Western Sectors. The Western Powers issued a declaration on 14 December, stating that they 'found unacceptable a unilateral repudiation by the Soviet Government of its obligations to the Governments of France, the United Kingdom and the United States in relation to their presence in Berlin and the freedom of access to the city'.

Geneva Conference
After the Soviet Union had let the six-month time limit that it had set in the Khrushchev-Ultimatum for the fulfilment of its demands expire, the Four Powers agreed to hold a conference of the Council of Foreign Ministers in 1959 in Geneva. The conference deliberated the German and Berlin questions without result and the Soviet Union categorically rejected all attempts to include East Berlin in discussions.

Kennedy and Khrushchev
At his meeting with US President John F. Kennedy in 1961 in Vienna, the Soviet Prime Minister announced that the Soviet Union would conclude a separate peace treaty with the GDR by the end of the year giving the GDR sovereignty over the communications lines to and from Berlin. There was little more the West could do, and within a few weeks the Soviet plans to divide artificially the East from the West were laid and the World's most infamous frontier was established. It was to survive for nearly three decades.

The Wall comes down
The removal of the Wall was in fact preceded by a lifting of frontier restrictions by Hungary in September 1989 when East Germans flooded into the west through Austria. People-power in Leipzig and Dresden spread to other areas of East Germany and grew into spontaneous demonstrations. There seemed to be no stopping the cry for freedom but it required a nod from Moscow, just as it had for Austria's independence in 1955. This duly came from President Mikhail Gorbachev.

German unification
At midnight on 2 October 1990 the German dream finally came true and after forty-five years of division the nation was united. East Germany had suffered a painful death and the German frontier in the east was again with Poland - the famous Oder-Neisse Line (see chapter 9). Unification was

hurried through under Article 23 of the West German constitution and a new Germany was born.

No peace treaty had been possible under two Germanies but a 'Treaty on the Final Settlement' was drawn up by the four Allied nations plus the two Germanies (the 'Two Plus Four') for formal ratification by each country's parliament. The Allied powers, however, suspended their rights ahead of unification day and the Soviet Union received $4 billion of West German aid to finance the withdrawal and resettlement of its 370,000 troops in East Germany. The last Soviet soldier is due to leave German soil by the end of 1994 after nearly fifty years of occupation.[11]

4

TRANSYLVANIA'S DISPUTED FRONTIERS

One of the secret treaties, or agreements, made during the First World War between Britain, France, Italy and Russia provided for the transfer of Transylvania from Hungary to Romania. However, the treaties of peace (1919-23)[1] which redrew the national frontiers after the break-up of the Austro-Hungarian and Ottoman Empires failed to accommodate the aspirations and hopes of all minority groups, numbering some 110 million people. This number, although considerably reduced, still amounts today to about 14 million or 10 per cent of the population,[2] and it is estimated that there are two million Hungarians in Transylvania. After the Romanian revolution in 1989 the lid was lifted off Transylvania's ancient rivalries and people have been living in a state of ethnic tension.

The Treaty of Peace between the Principal Allied and Associated Powers and Hungary was signed at Trianon, Versailles, on 4 June 1920. Hungary lost more than half her territory, including Transylvania to Romania and Western Hungary (now Burgenland) to Austria.[3]

The re-drawing of ethnic and linguistic frontiers in East Europe illustrated the weakness and irrelevance of the ideas which had inspired the Paris peace settlement at which seeds of great potential discord were sown, only to surface after fifty years of Nazi and Communist oppression. It is true that Lloyd George, in his memorandum to the Peace Conference, warned that there would never be peace in 'South-Eastern Europe' if every little state coming into being was to have a large 'Magyar Irredenta' within its borders. He suggested, therefore, that, as a guiding principle of the peace, as far as humanly possible the different races should be allocated to their mother-lands. In fact, the Treaty of Trianon transferred nearly one million Hungarians to Czechoslovakia, half a million to Yugoslavia and one and a half million to Romania, a total of one-third of the population of Hungary.

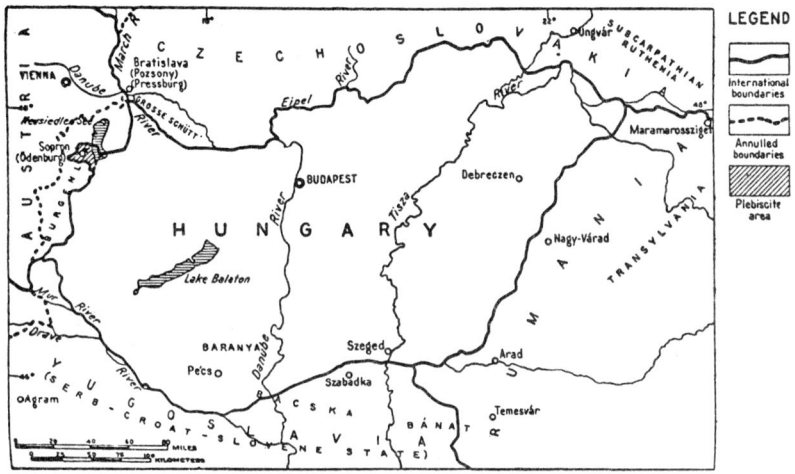

The Treaty of Trianon

The ceding of Burgenland to Austria seemed to be a concession to Austrian demands at the Peace Conference. In spite of a strong Hungarian protest based on the fact that the area depended for its wheat and flour and cattle on the Hungarian Plain to the east and that the presence of German colonists did not constitute a reason for transfer of the territory, the area was ceded to Austria by both the Austrian Treaty and the Treaty of Trianon. The city of Sopron in West Hungary, however, remained in Hungary by a plebiscite in 1921 (see chapter 28).[4] In addition to the loss of Transylvania and Burgenland, Hungary was also required to cede Bratislava, the Grosse Schutte and Slovakia to Czechoslovakia, and part of the Bánát and Hungarian Plain to the new state of Yugoslavia. The peace-makers of 1920 anticipated that in time these cessions of territories of the ethnic linguistic Hungarians would merge into the enclaves of the new frontiers, but they could not foresee the coming of Nazism and Communism.

Nor was the change which swept Eastern Europe in 1988-9 anticipated by today's politicians. It began in Hungary, the scene of the unsuccessful uprising in 1956, when Soviet troops surrounded Budapest and launched a massive surprise attack with an estimated 200,000 troops and 2,500 tanks and armoured cars. These fledgling democracies are now rebuilding their societies and in doing so face many problems - unemployment, high inflation, and old and new social and cultural tensions. Such conditions can ignite extremist political and ethnic rivalries and age old border disputes.

Transylvania is one such region, where it is reported that during 1990 some 35,000 refugees fled the region to Hungary because of reported repression.

In February 1990 the sinister Vatra Romaneasca movement was formed by professionals in defence of Romanians when trouble erupted in the schools in Tirgu Mures - a city where a population of 180,000 is split evenly between the two ethnic groups. Hungarian flags began to appear on schools where the Hungarian language replaced Romanian. The schools issue resulted in a demonstration against the Hungarians in Tirgu Mures in March 1990 when thousands gathered in the city.[5] The demonstration grew into a conflict in which five people were killed and 269 injured, two-thirds being Romanians. Other demonstrations in other parts of Transylvania have become commonplace, including one to mark the Vienna Decision of 1940 when Hitler transferred a large part of Transylvania to Hungary. This area was returned to Romania after the Second World War but in turn Romania ceded Besarabia and northern Bucovina to the Soviet Union.

Whilst freedom of the press was suppressed until the overthrow of the Communist regime, the running sore in Hungary since the Treaty of Trianon has never healed. On the 70th anniversary of the treaty, on 4 June 1990, the popular Budapest papers *Pesti Hirlap* and *Magyar Hirlap* for the first time ran leading articles critical of the treaty which moved Hungary's frontiers. The main problem area, however, is in Transylvania where, under extreme tension, Romanians see Hungarians as arrogant and overbearing and refer to them as 'Bosgors', or persons without a home. Few Hungarians, however, bother to hide the superiority they feel towards the Romanians and insist that Romania is not yet ready for democracy since the people have lived so long under oppression that they can be easily led.

There is little doubt that people in Transylvania are suffering post-revolution depression and the queues at shops are the same as in Ceausescu's time, the only difference being they can complain about it now. From border towns throughout Western Romania, people do their shopping in Hungary although queuing at the frontier takes anything up to twelve hours. Most Hungarians in Transylvania might admit that it is culture and language that define a nation and not its physical frontiers, but autonomy is necessary to preserve these beliefs and frontiers may require to be redrawn to gain that autonomy.[6]

5

CZECHOSLOVAKIA'S HISTORIC FRONTIERS

The State of Czechoslovakia was born after the First World War when the Austrian-Hungarian Empire was dismembered under the 1919 Treaty of Versailles. The frontiers of Czechoslovakia were determined under Article 82 of the treaty:[1]

> The old frontier as it existed on August 3 1914 between Austria-Hungary and the German Empire will constitute the frontier between Germany and the Czecho-Slovak State.

The stability of the 70-year-old country is today under threat, with claims of self-determination made by both the Czech region (Bohemia and Moravia) and the Slovak region.

The frontiers of Czechoslovakia were in fact based on the historical boundaries of Bohemia, Moravia and Austrian Silesia. At the Paris Peace Conference the Czechoslovakian delegation was opposed to any plebiscite to determine the frontiers of the Czech state. Their claim was that the Czech state had never ceased to exist and that it was the uncontested heir to the whole of the three provinces which had formerly constituted part of it. Their claim to the whole of the ancient Czech lands could be supported only on the argument of historic right and geographical unity, for a plebiscite would obviously have enabled the strong Polish and German majorities in various areas to prevent the setting up of the new state. The basis of their territorial claims was therefore the historical borders of these three provinces, but this apparently did not exclude the possibility of adding, on ethnic grounds, neighbouring regions in Prussia, Silesia in Lower Austria and the whole of Slovakia.

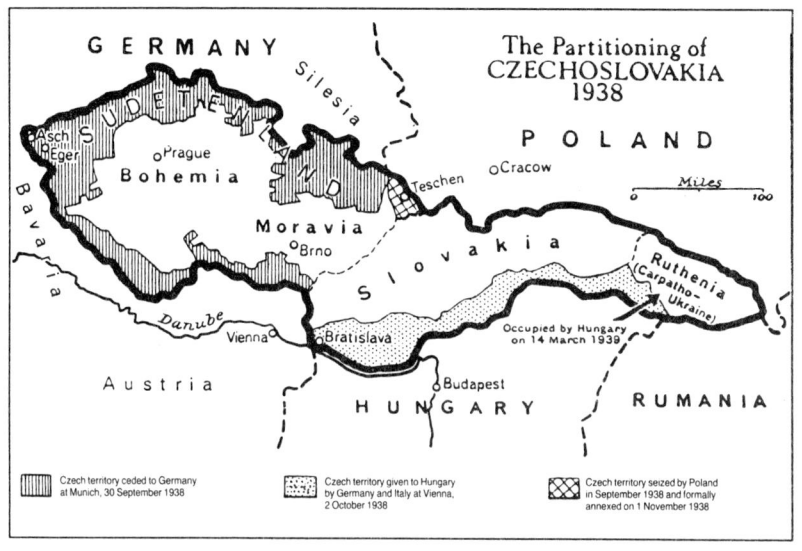

The new frontiers of Europe were in theory to be based on President Wilson's Fourteen Points (see Appendix) which essentially were designed to establish the right of national self-determination. Unfortunately the principle was not applied to national minorities who found themselves included in the new state of Czechoslovakia as well as other new states set up by the Peace Treaty. Newly revised nationalist sentiments led to considerable restriction of the rights of German minorities particularly in Czechoslovakia. This situation ultimately led to war in 1939 when German troops crossed the frontier on 1 October 1938 and marched into the Czechoslovakian Sudetenland breaking the undertaking Hitler had given to Chamberlain a few days before at Munich. The Sudeten Germans had of course been part of the Habsburg Empire and German was their mother tongue.

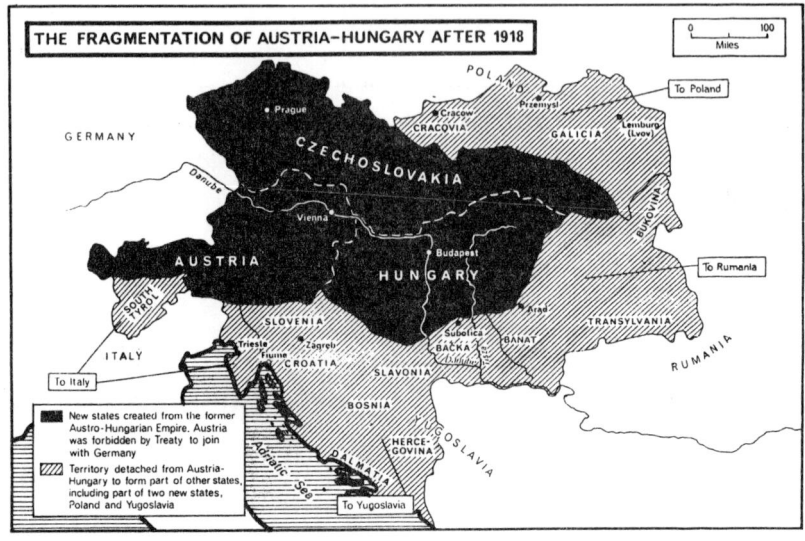

In 1919, out of 14 million people in the new state some 3 million were German and were concentrated in the border areas. However, Czech and German were utterly inter-dependent and no line on the ground could be drawn between the two populations. Despite the language difference, all were citizens of Czechoslovakia. However, every town and village was required to have a Czech or Slovak name, and Czech language tests for civil servants were made deliberately difficult. Germans were removed from public service, but there were schools and libraries for the German minority and German representatives in the national assembly. This area is now known as Bohemia (Bohem). During the Second World War national minorities were suppressed by the Nazis and after the war nationalistic passions were kept in check by Communism. Inspired by the memories of 1968 when reform was squashed by Soviet troops, the people of Prague staged massive protests in November 1989 to end forty-five years of Stalinist repression. Democracy, however, has encouraged nationalism to rise to the surface and in the Slovakian capital, Bratislava, demonstrations for autonomy are held almost daily.

A major irritant concerns the 600,000 ethnic Hungarians

who are required to use Slovak in dealing with public authorities.² These people were literally enclosed in the new state when the frontiers were established with Austria-Hungary according to the 1919 treaty (see chapter 4). Although the Slovaks number some 5 million or 30 per cent of the total population, free expression since the overthrow of the Communist regime has opened up long-festering wounds. The Slovaks also maintain that they have had a worse life than the Czechs in Bohemia or Moravia. Ironically, the language problem of the Slovaks is not directed against the Czechs, since the two languages are mutually comprehensible, but they want Slovak to be the only official language in an autonomous Slovakia.³ Their target is the Hungarian minority who, they say, enjoy generous educational and cultural linguistic rights. If political compromise cannot be negotiated, the regional frontiers of Czechoslovakia may yet require to be redrawn to satisfy ethnic and cultural nationalism.⁴

6

THE DISPUTED FRONTIERS OF AUSTRIA

After the First World War, in the draft peace treaty handed to the Austrian delegation on 2 June 1919 at St Germain-en-Laye near Paris, Austria lost Bohemia, Moravia, Austrian Silesia, South Tirol, Carniola (Krain), Southern Styria and southern Carinthia.[1] These areas had been ceded outright by Austria to the Allies for their subsequent disposal. The head of the Austrian delegation, Karl Renner, in a note of 10 June, protested that this would put millions of Austrians under foreign domination against their will and against their culture and economic interest. In a further note dated 15 June he referred to the Wilson principles (see Appendix) and asked that German Bohemia and the Sudetic country be allowed, as they themselves requested, to elect a constitutional assembly in each province to settle finally the fate of the people they represented. On the following day, Renner asked for plebiscites in the German speaking parts of Bohemia, Moravia and Austrian Silesia, in the mixed districts of the Tirol south of the Brenner, in Styria and Carniola (now Slovenia) and in parts of Carinthia ceded by the treaty to Yugoslavia.

These protests were repeated several times to no avail, except in the case of Carinthia. The Commission on Yugoslav Affairs recognised that southern Carinthia was an economic and geographic part of Austria and that all its economic relations were with the north. However, because of pressure from the Yugoslav leaders and the fact that according to Yugoslav statistics a majority of the people were Slovene speaking, it could reach no unanimous decision, and the Supreme Council, in the face of division among the experts, finally agreed to hold a plebiscite. This was held on 10 October 1920, a day that is still celebrated in Austria, and resulted in a majority vote in favour of Carinthia remaining in Austria by 22,025 votes to 15,278.²

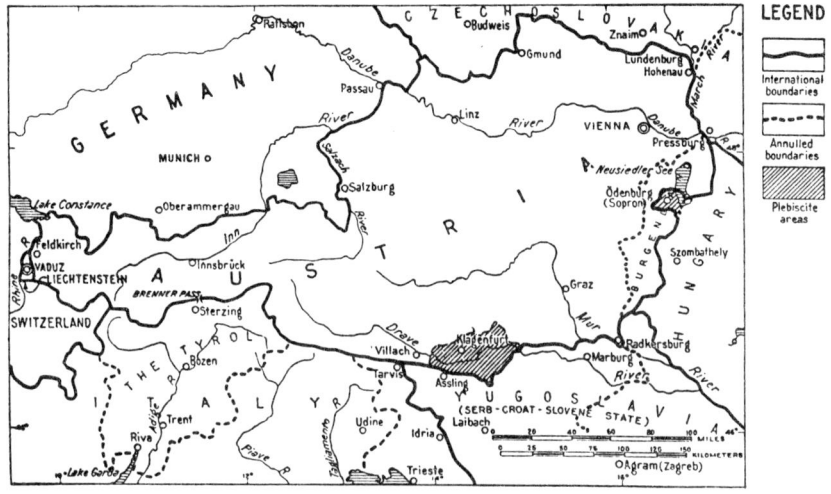

The Treaty of St. Germain-En-Laye

In the case of South Tirol, most of the region was both linguistically and culturally a part of Austria. However, a secret Treaty signed in London on 26 April 1915 between Britain, France, Russia and Italy secured Italy's entrance into the war on the Allied side by the promise of South Tirol, Trieste, Gorizia, most of Istria, northern Dalmatia and the Dodecanese (see chapter 10). By the Treaty of London, therefore, South Tirol was ceded to Italy and the Austria-Italy frontier, which at its extremity was moved some 90 miles north, was redrawn.

In the case of Carinthia, which was occupied by British forces after the Second World War, minority clauses for Slovene speakers in the Treaty of St Germain ensured a satisfactory arrangement which has been carefully adhered to by Austria. This stiuation was only in danger at the end of the Second World War when Tito's forces occupied southern Carinthia and claimed the territory for a brief spell until they were forced out by the British under protest. The frontier claimed by Yugoslavia and the plebiscite zone boundary is marked today by a tablet on the Villach-Faak road, and the 70th anniversary of the plebiscite was held in Klagenfurt on 10 October 1990 in the presence of the Austrian Chancellor and dignitaries from Yugoslavia. Yugoslavia, however, has never renounced her claim on southern Carinthia, and with Slovenia attaining independence, this now dormant claim may well be resurrected.

The Carinthian Question

South Tirol, however, after seventy years still remains a sensitive issue in Austria.[3] In spite of American President Wilson's fourteen points, it seems certain that the President knew the contents of the secret Treaty of London (and also of the secret treaty concerning Transylvania) as early as April 1917, but attached little importance to it, feeling confident that it would be rendered inoperative by the entrance of the United States into the war later that year. This, he thought, would cause the European Allies to yield. Wilson's principle of self-determination, however, applied to Germany, but had no effect on the South Tirol problem, in spite of the fact that Austria-Hungary had asked for a peace based on these principles and particularly based on Point 10 which stated that Austria-Hungary 'should be accorded the freest opportunity of autonomous development'. Italy, however, referred to Point

9 which demanded 'a readjustment of the frontiers of Italy along clearly recognizable lines of nationality' and claimed that geographic, strategic and historical considerations should enter into the drawing of the new frontiers. Italy claimed that:[4]

> The Italian Government considers that the 'readjustment' mentioned in Point 9 does not imply a mere rectification of frontiers; but that it means that Italy shall obtain the liberation of the provinces whose nationality is Italian, and at the same time shall establish a frontier between Italy and Austria-Hungary, or the other states which until now have formed part of Austria-Hungary, that offers the essential conditions of military security sufficient to assure independence and the maintenance of peace, in view of geographic and historic factors, and with the application of the same principles as those affirmed in the case of Germany in the matter of territorial elimination consequent upon the present.

While the United States delegation were of the opinion that the Wilson principles applied equally to Germany and Austria, the European Allies did not agree and recognised the Italian claim in accordance with the Treaty of London. However, this divergence of opinion regarding South Tirol appears to have been of little consequence. President Wilson made no effort to oppose the new frontier, although it is believed that Lloyd George and Clemenceau, the French Prime Minister, considered their hands tied by the London Treaty and hoped that he would. Thus, as the Treaty of London had provided, the Tirol up to and beyond the Brenner Pass as well as Kanaltal (Val Canale) to a few miles south of Villach, was taken from Austria outright and handed to Italy.

When Hitler added Austria to the Greater German Reich, many Austrians believed, and indeed hoped, that he would return South Tirol to Austria. It was a forlorn hope, however, mainly because of his commitment to Mussolini. Instead he arranged for those Austrians living under Italian rule in South

Tirol to continue to be re-housed in Tirol if they so wished. Some took up his offer but many remained as part of a strong ethnic and cultural group in South Tirol.

After the Second World War a further effort was made to unite South Tirol with Austria at the same time as the Austria-Yugoslav frontier was under dispute, and many demonstrations and minor conflicts took place. But while the Carinthian frontier was again secured for Austria, South Tirol eventually passed out of the political arena until 1991, the year when the wave of nationalism swept across Europe (see chapter 10).[5] Details of the actual delineation of the Italian-Yugoslav-Austrian frontiers as they now exist based on the Wilson, Morgan, and Rapallo Lines are given in chapter 10.

7

THE ATTILA LINE

The Attila Line delineates the 'frontier' separating the Turkish Cypriot Zone in the north of the island of Cyprus from the southern Greek Cypriot Zone.

Britain took over the administrative control of Cyprus in 1878 at the invitation of the Sultan of the Ottoman Empire as protection against Russian encroachment. The Greek Cypriots welcomed the occupation hoping for better government and prosperity, and under various High Commissioners were not disappointed. Britain introduced a new English legal system and a legislative council, and swept away outmoded methods of government including tax collection. By 1930 they had constructed some 3,000 miles of new roads and water supply and irrigation systems on the island.

Although the Cypriots ultimately became far from satisfied with British colonial rule, the only disturbance of any consequence was in 1931 when a growing desire for *enosis* (Union with Greece) developed. A plebiscite in 1950 organised by the then Bishop Kituim (Makarios) produced a 96 per cent majority for *enosis*. In 1955 the British Government invited Greece and Turkey to a tripartite conference (some 80 per cent of the population are Greek and 18 per cent Turkish). The conference failed, but by accepting Turkish participation at the conference, Greece gave a tacit recognition of Turkish rights in Cyprus. This did not prevent conflict between the parties and widespread violence erupted during 1955-6, led by EOKA an underground organisation which brought harsh disciplinary measures to the country and forced the temporary exile of Archbishop Markarios, by then head of the Independent Orthodox Church in Cyprus and leader of *enosis*.[1]

In 1959 conflict gave way to an agreement signed by Britain and Greek and Turkish Cypriot leaders under which Cyprus would become a republic with a president elected from the ethnic Greek community and a vice-president from the Turkish community. The proportion of Greek to Turkish representation in government would be two to one. Makarios was duly elected president and independence was declared in 1960. Cyprus joined the Commonwealth, the United Nations and the Council of Europe.

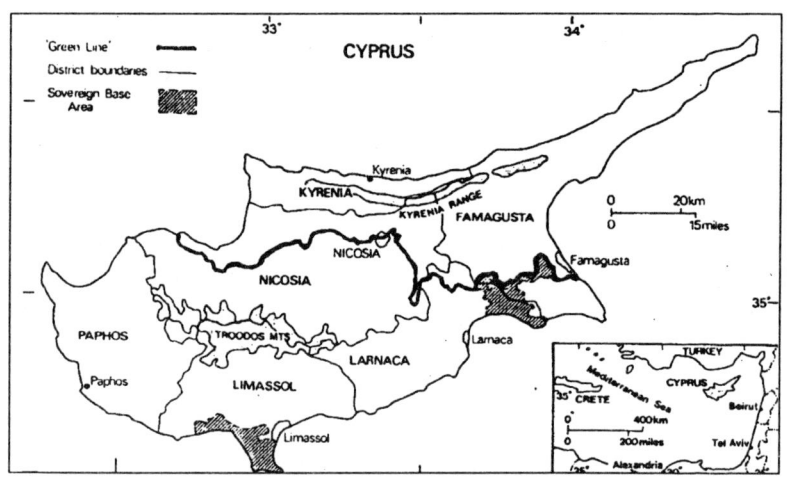

Cyprus: The Attila (Green) Line

However, just three years later communal fighting broke out due to Turkish complaints against the proposed new constitution and in 1964 a UN peace-keeping force was necessary to prevent an outbreak of war. This did not prevent fighting and war was prevented only by the mediation of the United States. Makarios was re-elected president in 1973, but a year later had to flee the country as the Cypriot National Guard, led by Greek troops, seized power with the long-term objective of *enosis* and named Nikes Sampson as the new president.

On 20 July, 1974, 6,000 Turkish troops with armoured and airborne units and aided by naval cover, invaded the country and within two days a further 25,000 troops were landed on the island. The invaders first took control of the 12 mile long Nicosia-Kyrenia highway and territory up to 15 miles deep on each side.

Although Greece mobilised its forces, it did not intervene, and a cease-fire was agreed on 22 July. At a meeting in Geneva between Britain, Greece and Turkey a week later a buffer zone was accepted by the two sides, to be controlled by a UN peace-keeping force. A few weeks later, a second peace conference at Geneva collapsed, fighting resumed and Turkish forces occupied the northern third of the island with each side charging the other with atrocities. The Turkish forces consolidated their position north and east from the Kyrenia bridgehead and ultimately took control of all territory north of a line running from Famagusta in the east to Lefta in the west. This line became the frontier between the Turkish Cypriot Zone and the Greek Cypriot Zone and was later known as the Attila Line (also commonly referred to as the Green Line, Red Line or Sahin Line).

The fighting left behind 200,000 refugees from a population of only 600,000. Some 10,000 Turkish Cypriots in the Greek controlled south were flown to the northern zone from British bases and 200,000 Greeks were expelled from the Turkish controlled north to be replaced by thousands of Turks from the mainland. A unilateral declaration of independence was announced by Turkish Cypriots in 1983 and the new state was named the Turkish Republic of Northern Cyprus.

The several UN resolutions over the years calling upon Turkey to withdraw its forces from the island and respect the independence of Cyprus, all failed. Many proposals were discussed with the US, the UN and the Commonwealth without success.[2]

Owing to the entrenched position adopted by each side, no compromise seems likely in the near future. Visitors to the island are faced with movement restrictions imposed by one side or the other and formal permission must be obtained in order to pass from the Greek Zone into the Turkish Zone. Access is permitted only at certain points as the island continues to be divided by the Attila Line.

8

THE GREEN LINE

The 'Green Line', as it has come to be known since it was established in 1975, divided Beirut into Christian and Moslem zones with the sole hazardous crossing-point at the National Museum. The 5 mile long line was accepted by the people of the city as a fact of life, as real to the Lebanese as the Berlin Wall to the Germans.

The museum crossing-point was always a daily hazard for those whose work required them to go back and forth between East and West across the line. By a tacit arrangement, each morning witnessed a truce while newspapers were passed each way through the crossing-point. The Arab peace-keeping force endeavoured to keep the checkpoint open for most of the time and Saudi soldiers held a 200 yard stretch of highway on the Moslem side of the line even when mortar or shells fell all around them. A bend in the road at the crossing-point was considered a dangerous trouble spot for each side because it denied direct observation from the white-helmeted peace troops.

The establishment of the Green Line saw the start of fifteen years of bloody civil war in Lebanon between complex factions, mainly between Christians and Moslems but including from time to time Palestinians, Phelange Maromite militia, Druse and Shiite militia.

In the first nineteen months the war claimed 60,000 victims and caused considerable damage to the infrastructure of the country. Palestinians and leftist Moslems fought Maromite militia, the Phalange and other Christians. Support for the various factions came from several Arab countries while the Christian forces were aided by Israel.

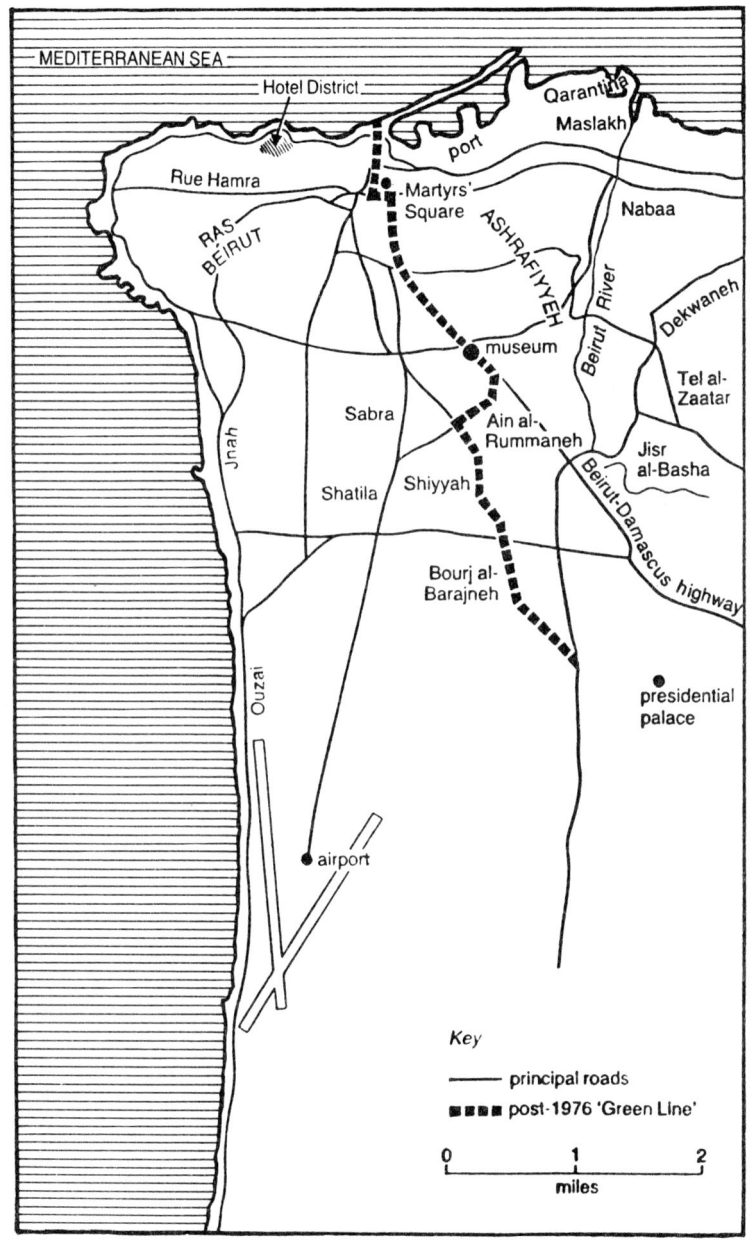

Beirut: The Green Line

In 1976 some 15,000 Syrian troops intervened and fought Palestinian groups. Through the years cease-fires came and went, and the fighting continued even between similar ethnic and religious groups like Moslem against Moslem.

Israeli forces invaded in 1982 in a land, sea and air attack to destroy enclaves of the Palestine Liberation Organisation (PLO), and in spite of Syrian opposition in the Bekaa Valley, Beirut was encircled by Israeli troops (see chapter 2). Some 4,000 PLO followers with their leader Yasir Arafat evacuated Beirut after having fought, with the backing of Syria, a bloody six-week battle in Tripoli.

Today Israel still maintains a 9 mile deep buffer zone in southern Lebanon for security against guerilla attacks, an area which Syria, with her 40,000 troops in Lebanon, acknowledges and accepts. However, there are more armed Palestinian guerillas in southern Lebanon today than when Israel invaded Lebanon. Terrorist bombing in the Lebanon became a way of life. In one such explosion in 1983 at the US Embassy 50 people were killed, and 241 US troops and 58 French soldiers died in separate Moslem suicide attacks. Kidnapping of foreign nationals by Islamic militants became common throughout the eighties and British, US, French and even Soviet citizens have fallen victim of this diabolical crime.

On 18 October 1990, after a ferocious weekend battle, the Green Line was suddenly bulldozed into the history books, but not before some 700 people were killed and more than 1,000 wounded. Syrian bulldozers flattened the structures of the Line and cleared hundreds of explosive devices planted over the 15 years of fighting. Once a haven for snipers, the line was immediately crossed by hundreds of motorists and pedestrians, many of whom had waited since 1983 to make the East-West crossing. It was in 1983 that the restrictions were first lifted for a brief period and the city centre somewhat restored until fighting closed the crossing points again.[1]

Many Lebanese, therefore, have a pessimism, born of dashed hopes for peace, but some are encouraged that this time peace in Lebanon is not far off. The Christians may have been defeated by their rival Moslems and Syrians, but a realistic medium between the optimists' euphoria and the pessimists' depression may have at last been reached.

9

THE ODER-NEISSE LINE

Poland's history dates from 966 and it was a great power from the 14th to 17th centuries. In three partitions (1772, 1793, 1795) the country was apportioned between Prussia, Russia and Austria, and in 1795 disappeared from the map to reappear in 1809 as the Grand Duchy of Warsaw. In the First World War Poland was overrun by the Austro-German armies but its independence was recognised by the Treaty of Versailles (1919). In the invasion by Germany on 1 September 1939, which triggered the Second World War, it was annexed by Germany. It was then divided between Germany and the Soviet Union when, two weeks after the German invasion, the Soviets invaded from the east.

After the Second World War, in accordance with decisions made by the Allies at Yalta, and later confirmed at Potsdam, Poland's frontiers were once again moved. The western frontier with Germany was drawn along the Oder and Neisse Rivers, later to be know as the Oder-Neisse Line. This frontier added former German territories that included the rest of Silesia and Pomerania and the southern portion of East Prussia that contained Masuria.[1] The frontier was originally provisional pending a post-war peace treaty, and was disputed by Germany's right-wing political parties who urged that Germany reclaim these territories.[2] But in June 1990 the Parliaments of the two Germanies, East and West, adopted matching resolutions guaranteeing that the Oder-Neisse Line would remain as the official frontier. This became a delicate situation, however, just before, and immediately after, German unification in October 1990. The treaty which finally confirmed the forty-five year old disputed frontier was duly signed by Poland and a united Germany a few months later on 14 November.[3]

The Oder-Neisse Line and Poland's territorial adjustments

The demarcation of a frontier line cannot avoid having anomalies and the Oder-Neisse Line is no exception. An example concerns the former all German city of Goerlitz which was split by the River Neisse, the west bank going to Germany and the east bank to Poland. The Polish part of the city changed its name to Zgorzelec and the frontier between the two parts of the city was crossed by the river bridge. Incidents were common, especially during the run-up to German unification, and indeed the frontier was virtually closed for many years after the Second World War.

The frontier also bisects the old German city of Frankfurt an der Oder, the east bank now being known as Slubice. In the run-up to German unification here, blood red swastikas were daubed on pubs in Slubice and slogans and Nazi salutes were incitements to riot. Germans who had been dispossessed when the frontier was clumsily drawn were talking about the return of Silesia, Pomerania and Prussia.[4]

In Kostrzyn thousands of German exiles searched through dusty town hall files to find their birth certificates to prove their German ancestry and boasted that this time there would be no invasion of Silesia – they would just buy it.[5]

The Oder-Neisse Line acquired for Poland some 40,000 square miles of German territory by moving the frontier west in compensation for the loss of some 77,000 square miles to the Soviet Union in the east including the loss of Vilnius and Lvov (see chapter 16). The Atlantic Charter had been conveniently ignored (see Appendix).

In addition, the part of Cieszyn Silesia seized by Poland in 1938, was returned to Czechoslovakia.[6]

10

THE WILSON, THE RAPALLO AND THE MORGAN LINES

The problem of the delineation of the Italian frontiers (Italy-Austria; Italy-Yugoslavia) was one of the most difficult matters with which the Peace Conference had to deal after the First World War.[1] In the case of the Italy-Yugoslav frontier after the Second World War, final agreement was not reached until nine years after the war. Two proposed lines dominated the negotiations – the Wilson Line (after US President Woodrow Wilson) after the First World War, and the Morgan Line (after General Morgan, Chief of Staff to Field Marshal Alexander in Italy) after the Second World War. As it happened neither line was the final one agreed, but in each case the lines offered a solution for discussion and negotiation, and in the end the frontiers corresponded to them quite closely.

However, after the First World War, there were in all six possible frontiers to be considered by the Allies, namely:

The pre-1914 frontier
The London Treaty Line (April 1915)
The Italian claim at the Peace Conference (March 1919)
The Yugoslav claim at the Peace Conference (April 1919)
The Wilson Line (1919)
The Treaty of Rapallo Line (November 1920)

The northern frontier of Italy with Austria is dealt with in chapter 6. Of main concern was South Tirol, where the districts of Trentino and Alto Adige were the areas under dispute after the First World War. The area of the former is 2,454 square miles and of the latter 2,953 square miles. The counties of Trent (Trient) and Bozen (Bolzano) were under the temporal rule of the Prince-Bishop of Trent from the middle ages until their secularization in 1803 and final annexation to Tirol in 1814. The Austrian Emperor at the same time annexed the adjacent counties of Brixen and Vistgau (Val Venosta). All had in practice been under Habsburg influence or control for some centuries.

Napoleon took the Alto Adige and Trentino area from Austria and included it in his kingdom of North Italy under the name of Alto Adige. The Trentino was wholly Italian or at least Romance, for there were Ladins as well as Italians. On the other hand there was, and still is, an Austria preponderance in Alto Adige. In the Austrian census of 1910 there were 13,450 Austrians in Trentino but over 360,000 Italians and Ladins; in Alto Adige there were over 215,000 Austrians and only 22,500 Italians and Ladins. It is no surprise therefore that Trentino had always been violently pro-Italian and the Alto Adige very much pro-Austrian. So the question was how could a frontier line reconcile both ethnic and strategic justice?

During the war, and before Italy entered the conflict, Austria-Hungary had discussed with Italy a new Austrian-Italian frontier in the event of Italy joining the Central Powers. Austria was prepared to sacrifice the Trentino but not Alto Adige as was proposed in the new frontier. No agreement could be reached, and instead Italy signed the Treaty of London with the Great (Allied) Powers. The Treaty of London proposed a frontier giving Italy both Trentino and Alto Adige and also delineated the Italy-Yugoslavia frontier as follows:[2]

> The frontier shall be traced as follows (Article 4 of the London Treaty):
> From Piz Umbrail as far as north of the Stelvia, it shall follow the crest of the Rhetian Alps up to the sources of the Adige and Eisach, then following the Reschen and Brenner mountains and the Oetz and Ziller heights. The frontier shall then bend towards the south, cross Mt Toblach and join the present frontier of the Carnic Alps. It shall follow this frontier line as far as Mt Tarvis and from Mt

Tarvis the watershed of the Julian Alps by the Predil Pass, Mt Mangart, the Tricorno (Terglu) and the watersheds of the Podbendo, Podlaniscam and Idria passes. From this point the frontier shall follow a south-easterly direction towards the Schneeberg, leaving the entire basin of the Save and its tributaries outside Italian territory. From the Schneeberg the frontier shall come down to the coast in such a way as to include Castua, Mattuglia and Volosca within Italian territory.

This treaty article gave Italy Trentino, Cisalpine Tirol with its geographical and natural frontier (the Brenner frontier) as well as Trieste, Gorizia and Gradisca, all Istria as far as the Quarnero and including Volosca and the Istrian islands of Cherso and Lussin, as well as the small islands of Plavnik Unie, Canidale, Palazzuoli, San Pietro di Nembi, Asinello, Gruica and the neighbouring islets.

Under Article 5 Italy would also receive the province of Dalmatia and the Adriatic islands and, under Article 6, the Bay of Valona.

The South Tirol problem refuses to go away and as nationalism swept Europe in 1991, the lingering emotion of separation was once again aroused. The German Group in South Tirol has opposed Italian rule since 1919 but Mussolini strengthened Rome's authority by infusing Italian industry and workers into the province. The German language was barred and over 8,000 place names were Italianised. By the 1960s South Tirol extremists had engaged in over 100 arson attacks on government property and called for UN intervention in their bid for independence. One solution now being advocated is the formation of 'special status' regions for five of Italy's troubled regions – Alto Adige, Val d'Aosta, Fruili-Venezia-Giulia, Sardinia and Sicily. A massive demonstration held on the Brenner on 15 September pressed for a 'united Tirol' inside a Europe 'made up of regions'.

The Austria-Yugoslavia frontier problem is discussed in chapter 6. The matter became almost as serious for the Peace

Conference as the delineation of the Italy-Yugoslavia frontier. After the war in 1918, Yugoslavia contended that they were justified in adopting the line of the ethnic frontier which was considerably further north of the watershed of the Karawanken Alps. At the end of April 1919, the situation became so dangerous that the Yugoslavs, strengthened by Serbian troops, crossed the frontier and threatened the Klagenfurt Basin. By the end of May almost the whole basin was overrun and Klagenfurt captured with immense quantities of Austrian war materiel. On the demand of the Great Powers, both sides ceased hostilities and an armistice was signed on 6 June. On the 8 June, however, Austria resumed hostilities and Italian troops occupied the Villach-Feldkirch-St Veit railway on 13 June to safeguard routes to Vienna. The troops remained until after the plebiscite result was declared but an ultimatum was required to demand that the Yugoslavs withdraw their forces by 20 October which they duly did and the frontier returned to the watershed of the Karawanken. At the conference Italy claimed additional territory including Tarvis, the Kanaltal (Val Canale) and the Sexten Valley.

The Italy-Yugoslavia frontier, however, caused considerable disagreement. The Italians resented the idea that Croats and Slovenes, who had recently been fighting Italians, should now be regarded as Allies. Feelings ran high and parts of Yugoslav territory occupied by Italy were placed under a repressive Yugoslav regime caused the Allied Powers to refuse to accept any Yugoslav delegates to the conference. However, President Wilson responded by recognising the Serb-Croat-Slovene state (Yugoslavia) and the Yugoslav delegation duly appeared to present their case. The fixing of the frontier involved not only Venezia Giulia but Fiume (Rijeka), Trieste, Dalmatia and the Adriatic islands.

President Wilson proposed a line which gave Trieste, Pula (Pola) and the greater half of the Istrian peninsula to Italy, but followed northwards a geographical line to beyond Tarvis but south of Villach and gave Fiume to Yugoslavia. The frontier was, in places, as much as 20 miles west of the Treaty of London Line and was the subject of a heated objection by Italy. Deadlock resulted.

The Yugoslavs demanded a plebiscite for all the disputed areas and reported to the President of the Peace Conference (Council of Four) that informal plebiscites taken secretly had confirmed an anti-Italian result. But feelings were so high that the Italian delegation left the conference and returned to Italy claiming that Fiume was an ancient Italian city, that Dalmatia had been forcibly denationalized in recent years, and that the Treaty of London Line should be adhered to on the grounds of security.

In considering the Fiume-Dalmatia question with respect to ethnic, economic and strategic considerations, if the Treaty of London had been enforced some 365,000 Yugoslavs would have gone to Italy. If Fiume had gone to Yugoslavia, some 28,000 Italians (23,000 in Fiume) would have gone to Yugoslavia. The Wilson Line, on the other hand, gave Italy some 360,000 Yugoslavs but the Austrian census of 1910 gave only 18,000 Italians in Dalmatia and 600,000 Slavs. The facts of this situation were that while Italian brains, capital and enterprise had dominated the coast and towns in the Middle Ages, the population had seen the development of economic life among the Slavs and the consequent peaceful expulsion of Italian influence. The Slavs, once simple peasants, had become shopkeepers, shippers, and bankers and no longer needed Italian aid.

Italy's claim on northern Dalmatia centred on the military necessity of protecting the country from invasion. It had a strong case on strategic grounds for obtaining some island as a naval base since between Venice and Brindisi there was no good harbour on the Italian east coast. Dalmatia, on the other hand, abounded in excellent harbours which had in the past been the haunts of pirates and in 1919 could have been made the nests for submarines. Several islands were in fact suggested at the Peace Conference including Lissa, Lagosta, Pelagosa, Cattaro and Sebenico. With Pula and Valona and a central island base, Italy would carry the keys to the Adriatic.

The deadlock was broken by President Wilson when he made the great concession to Italy of the Brenner frontier on the understanding that Italy would modify her claim to her frontier with Yugoslavia. The proposed settlement was to create a temporary independent demilitarized zone or 'buffer state' under the League of Nations including the town of Fiume, the boundary approximating the Wilson Line. Although negotiations on this proposal broke down, it remained the basis for further schemes, again using either the Wilson Line, the Treaty of London Line, or a variation of each as Italy's eastern frontier. Fighting broke out in Fiume and troops had to be called out. Agreement seemed as far away as ever and the idea of a buffer state to solve the problem was dropped.

The President of the Council, the President of the United States and both Britain and France had failed to find a formula for agreement and Italy and Yugoslavia were at last left to work out their own solution which they duly did by the Treaty of Rapallo (1920). The Rapallo Line was a compromise and in general followed the Treaty of London Line from the Adriatic to Austria, joining the Austria-Italy-Yugoslavia frontier at Pec (sic). Full liberty and independence was given to the Free State of Fiume (population then 36,000, today 130,000).

Of the Istrian isles, Cherso and Lussin went to Italy and of the Dalmatian Islands, Italy retained only Lagosta and Pelagosa. The frontier across Istria favoured Italy and gave her about 470,000 Yugoslavs, but Dalmatia went to Yugoslavia. It is perhaps interesting to note that Italy was probably fortunate to obtain Tarvis and the Sexten Valley. In the Treaty of London, Article 4 (see above), and in the Armistice of 1918, Mt Tarvis is stated as a point of demarcation but no such mountain exists. It could be argued that the heights north or even south of the town were meant, a very great difference from the Austrian point of view since the pre-1914 frontier was 20 miles south of Tarvis. According to the Treaties of London, Rapallo and St Germain, the three frontiers met at a point 'Pec' or 'Pec Vfen' (4,950 ft). This name does not exist locally and is now known as Ofen or the Dreiländer Kreuz.

And so the Italian-Yugoslav frontier was at last delineated.

In only twenty-five years time, however, it was to be altered again, and substantially so.

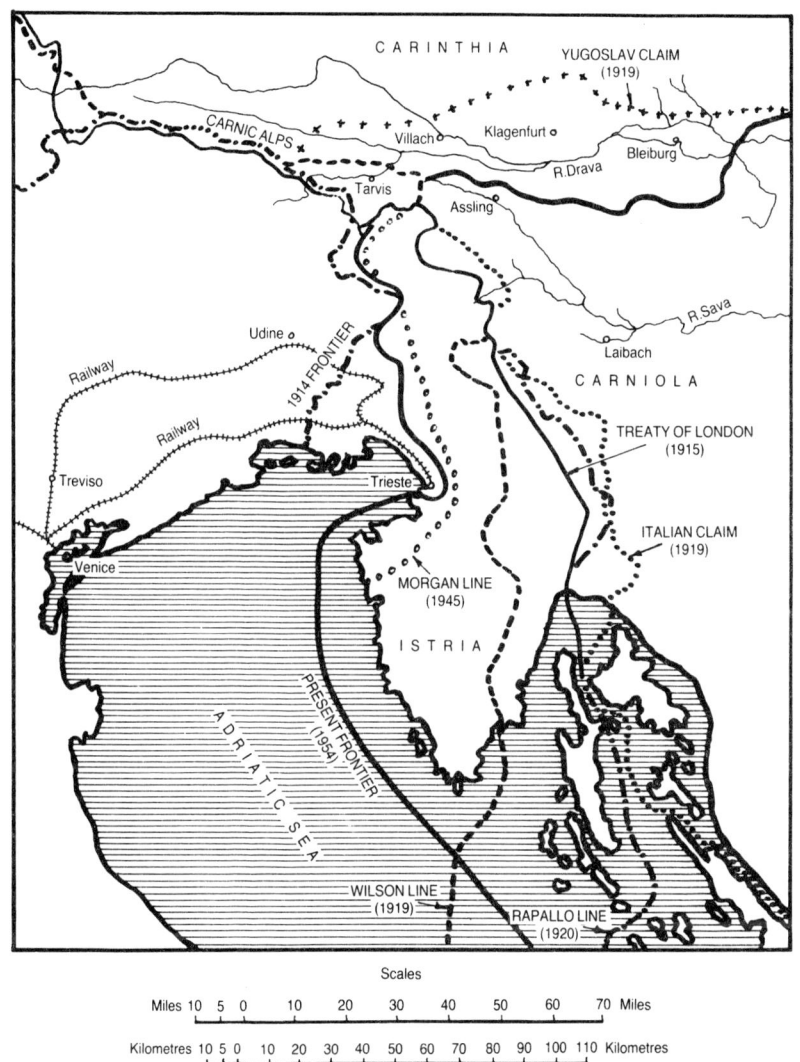

The Seven proposed lines to establish
the Italy-Yugoslavia frontier, 1914-1954

In the Spring of 1945, as the Second World War was drawing to a close, the British Eighth Army was racing Marshal Tito to Trieste and Klagenfurt. In Yugoslavian eyes the situation this time differed from 1918 because Tito was an ally and he demanded Venezia Giulia and southern Carinthia, the whole to be known as Greater Yugoslavia - and he declared that the Soviet Union supported his claims.

As the Second New Zealand Division entered Venezia Giulia they found the Yugoslavs already there, and when they raced into Trieste the Yugoslavs were there too. In Austria the British 5 Corps sped into Klagenfurt just a few hours before Tito's troops. Harold Macmillan said of the occasion in his diary:[3]

> The Yugoslavs were claiming part if not all of the Province of Carinthia. Believing possession to be nine-tenths of the law, they had raced us into Austria, just as they had raced us into Venezia Giulia. They actually reached Klagenfurt after us, so we had been able to secure the best buildings and put sentries in them. But we had not enough men to guard every place.

However, Tito's partisans were already in southern areas of Carinthia, where they had in fact been engaged in conflict with the enemy during the war. The partisans claimed with justification that Slovene Carinthia was the only province of the Greater German Reich which offered armed resistance to the Nazis.[4] Their repeated attacks against important lines of communication running across Carinthia hindered the movement of troops and war materiel and tied down large units of the German army.

During the war it is believed that over 3,500 Yugoslav partisans fought in Carinthia of which 80 per cent were Slovene Carinthians. The first units were formed as early as 1942 and in the Spring of 1943 the first Slovene Carinthian Partisan battalion was formed. Later, a few Austrian battalions joined the struggle and units conducted sabotage from Tarvisio in the west to Styria in the east, but mainly concentrated around Unterdrauburg (Dravograd) and Marburg (Maribor). They claimed to have carried out over 600 military engagements against the enemy up to the end of the war, the enemy suffering some 9,000 killed, wounded or taken prisoner. The partisans reported losing over one thousand killed in action, 710 wounded and 317 taken prisoner or declared missing. Some 150 enemy garrisons were said to be in Carinthia during this period.

As well as partisan units operating in Carinthia, similar units were engaged in conflict and sabotage throughout Venezia Giulia, aided by British SOE units centred in Slovenia. The situation in Carinthia in May 1945 was becoming no less dangerous than Venezia Giulia as Tito threw more and more troops into the area. The British force was down to some 25,000 troops and the matter was now being dealt with at the highest political level. What made the situation even more serious was Tito's claim that the Soviet Government would back him in his request for part of the territory of Carinthia so as to move the present frontier some 25 miles north to include the towns of Villach and Klagenfurt.[5]

By the 16 May Field Marshal Alexander, C in C Army Headquarters in Italy, had instructed 15 Army Group to prepare a detailed plan of operations to expel Tito's forces from both Carinthia and Venezia Giulia. In addition to this problem Alexander also had to deal with the matter of some 70,000 Cossacks and 30,000 Anti-Tito Yugoslavs as well as over 500,000 refugees and German prisoners of war who had all gathered in the British Zone of Carinthia.

However, by 20 May the Governments of Britain, the US and the Soviet Union had reached an arrangement whereby Tito's forces would retire south of the 1939 frontier of the Karawanken and await the peace negotiations. In Venezia Giulia, again with all three Governments in agreement, Tito's forces retired behind a frontier line proposed by General Morgan. Negotiations on Trieste and Venezia Giulia, however, continued into June with the possibility of conflict leading to war ever imminent. On 9 June, just over five weeks after the fall of Trieste, Tito finally yielded and an agreement along the lines demanded by the Allies was signed in Belgrade.

The future of the frontiers of the whole region was to be a matter for the peace conference and meantime Venezia Giulia was divided into two zones, along the Morgan Line. Trieste, Gorizia, Monfalcone and the countryside up to and including the lines of communication to Austria became Zone A under direct Allied Military Administration. So too did Pula, but the rest of the province remained under Yugoslav control as Zone B. By 12 June Yugoslav evacuation to east of the Morgan Line was complete and Yugoslav control of Western Giulia and Trieste was at an end.

Although temporary agreements had been made on both the Austria-Yugoslavia frontier and the Italy-Yugoslavia frontier, arguments and wrangling persisted for some years more; in the case of the former frontier until 1948/49. In the latter case the settlement went through two main stages. Under the 1947 Treaty of Peace with Italy, Gorizia and Monfalcone went to Italy. Trieste and the coastal strip between it and the Isonzo River, and the area for 20 miles south towards Pula, became an independent Free Territory under the aegis of the United Nations. British and US troops remained in Trieste and British communications went through British Troops in Austria (BTA).

It became clear, however, that the Free Territory idea was not going to work and Marshal Tito agreed to a new frontier in 1954. Trieste and the coastal strip westwards to the Isonzo went to Italy but the coastal and hill areas to the south went to Yugoslavia. The new frontier to Austria was in places some 30 miles west of the 1920 Rapallo frontier but generally followed the Morgan Line. This frontier, although it has never had final legal agreement, has successfully stood the test of time and peaceful coexistence now reigns along its mountainous, tortuous line from the Adriatic to the Austrian border.[6]

11

THE 49TH PARALLEL

The United States and Canada share the longest undefended frontier in the world. There are no armies along this 5,500 mile border which has 96 legal crossings (and thousands of informal ones) used each year by more than a hundred million people.

The border, first surveyed by the British in 1774 to define the US-Canada frontier, bisects farms, country roads and houses. It was established by the Treaty of Ghent (1814) which provided for a restoration of all conquered territories. The treaty also provided for a commission to settle the disputed northeast frontier, but by mutual understanding the question of the Great Lakes and fisheries was left open for a future negotiation. The north-west frontier issue was settled in 1818 in London when it was fixed along the 49th parallel from the Lake of the Woods to the crest, or watershed, of the Rocky Mountains, thus recognising the northern line of the Louisiana Purchase (Louisiana was purchased by the US from France in 1803 for $15 million).

The controversial northeast frontier (Maine to New Brunswick) was fixed along its present line in 1842. The US received about 7,000 of the 12,000 square miles of disputed territory and the claims of Maine and Massachusetts were satisfied in part by a payment of $150,000 to each state. Also in 1842 the northern frontier of Vermont and New York west to the Lake of the Woods was agreed between Britain and the US. It was based on the 1774 surveys and adjusted about half a mile north of the 45th parallel.

In 1846 the US pressed its claim for the whole of Oregon

to the 54° 40' line of latitude which at that time was the Russian frontier of Alaska. The cry from the US was '54° 40' or fight'. However, because of the growing economic ties between the two nations, and the promise that Britain would refrain from interfering in the US-Mexico problem, a compromise was reached and a treaty agreed which provided that the frontier between the US-Canada (British territory in Oregon) would be an extension of the existing continental line along the 49th parallel to the middle of the channel between Vancouver Island and the mainland and thence along a line running southward through Juan de Fuca Strait to the Pacific. In the south, Mexico relinquished all claims to Texas above the Rio Grande and ceded California and New Mexico to the US in 1848. The total area ceded amounted to nearly 2 million square miles and included parts of Utah, Nevada, Arizona and Colorado. Florida (under Spanish rule, as far west as the Mississippi) was annexed in three stages – 1810, 1813 and 1819.[1]

The southern frontier of the United States was completed in 1853 by the purchase from Mexico by James Gadsden, appointed by the US to negotiate a boundary dispute concerning a strip of territory about 45,000 square miles in area in the Mesilla Valley south of the Gila River. Under the terms of the agreement, the US paid Mexico $10 million for the territory to be ceded. The line established marks the present frontier between the US and Mexico and became known as the Gadsden Purchase.

Alaska was considered by Russia as an economic liability and was sold in 1867 to the US for just over $7 million. In 1903 an Alaskan boundary dispute which arose after the Klondike gold rush of 1896 showed that the Alaskan Panhandle (lying in US territory) commanded the water routes to the goldfields. A joint commission meeting in London in the same year upheld the US claims, and the award ran a line which excluded Canada from ocean inlets of the Alaskan Panhandle, thus denying Canada free access to the Yukon goldfields.[2]

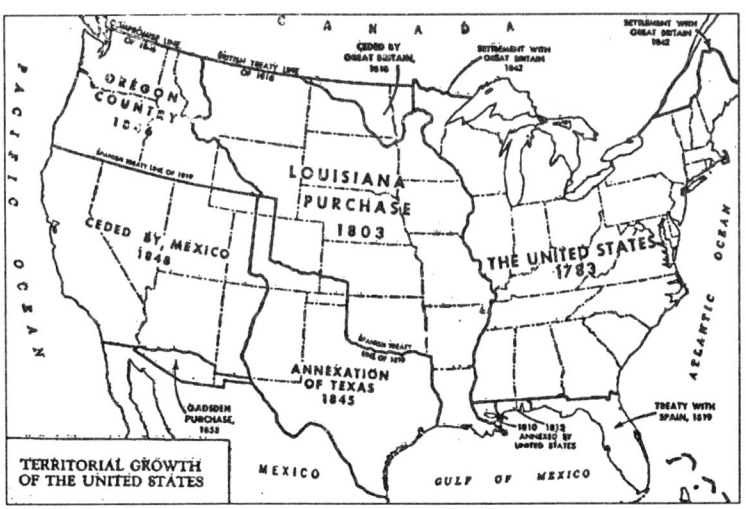

Canada recognises the 1903 frontier Agreement that crosses the northern tip of the Alaska Panhandle at latitude 54° 40 known as the AB Line (Alaska-British Columbia Line). The US claims, however, that the border runs as much as twenty-five miles further south, equidistant between the offshore islands of both nations, thus giving Alaskan fishermen legal access to rich fishing grounds in the Dixon Entrance, patrolled by US Coast Guard. Even today fishing rights remain an issue along the frontier as they do off the Atlantic coast. For some twenty years now each nation has sporadically seized the other's vessels and as recently as the summer of 1989 the US impounded two Canadian trawlers for alleged fishing in US waters. In one case the family who owned one of the boats had to post a $50,000 (US) bond to have their boat back. It was duly returned, less about $7,000 (US) worth of salmon.[3]

The long, invisible, unguarded line of the 49th Parallel has been defended successfully over the years by the sole garrison of trust and goodwill. It has helped greatly that Americans and Canadians speak the same language and have a general dislike of standing armies and navies. If there ever had been such military forces, war may well have resulted. It is probable that Canada's more divisive border may prove to be the ethnic and linguistic one between Quebec and the rest of the country.

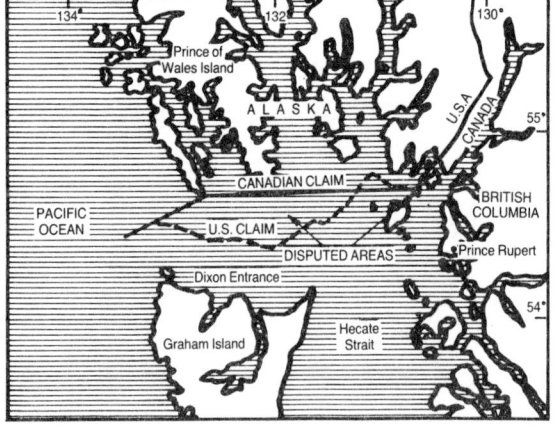

Disputed marine frontier between the United States and Canada

12

THE 17TH PARALLEL

From 111BC to 939AD Vietnam was held by Chinese peoples who in 1288 defeated the armies of Kublai Khan. French colonialism started in 1858 and ended in a French protectorate in 1884. In 1940 Vietnam was occupied by Japan, and at the end of the Second World War France attempted to restore its control in Indochina. However, in December 1946 French control was effectively challenged in Vietnam by a national resistance inspired by a native Communist leadership. In 1954 France suffered a decisive defeat at Dien Bien Phu, a name that arguably has come to symbolize the collapse of western imperialism.

At a conference of foreign ministers in 1954 in Geneva a provisional partition of Vietnam was agreed along the 17th parallel. The agreement provided for a buffer zone, a withdrawal of French troops from the North and elections to determine the country's future. Under the agreement the Communists gained control of territory north of the 17th parallel with twenty-two provinces in an area of 62,000 square miles and a population of 13 million with its capital at Hanoi and Ho Chi Minh as president. South Vietnam comprised thirty-nine provinces and a population of 12 million in an area of 65,000 square miles with its capital in Saigon. Some 900,000 North Vietnamese fled to the South but neither South Vietnam nor the United States signed the Geneva Accord. The following year the government of South Vietnam proclaimed the Republic of Vietnam.[1]

In 1959 the Democratic Republic of Vietnam in the North adopted a constitution based on Communist principles and called for the unification of all Vietnam. Conflict between North and South during the years from 1954 to 1959 led in 1964 to large scale troop infiltration, with the United States supplying aid to the South and China and the Soviet Union supplying the north.

Vietnam: The 17th Parallel

Beginning in 1965, when its troops became combatants, the United States stepped up air strikes and by the end of the war had dropped some 6 million tons of bombs. By 1969 the United States had a troop strength of over half a million in South Vietnam. However, following a series of withdrawals, ordered by President Nixon, a cease-fire was signed in Paris in 1973. It was never implemented and the United States curbed their involvement in the following year. North Vietnamese forces launched substantial attacks during the first months of 1975 and South Vietnam surrendered on 30 April. The 17th parallel ceased to be the frontier between North and South when the country was re-united in the following year, with Hanoi as its capital and the flag and anthem of North Vietnam unanimously adopted by the Socialist Republic. Saigon was re-named Ho Chi Minh City.

The toll of the ten years of the Vietnam war (1965-75) included nearly 48,000 US combat deaths and 200,000 South Vietnamese losses. Other allied forces lost over 5,000 men and there were over one million civilian casualties. Displaced war refugees in South Vietnam totalled some 6.5 million. The United States took over 165,000 refugees, and other countries some 100,000.

13

THE 38TH PARALLEL

Communist North Korea and capitalist South Korea, separated by the 38th parallel, are technically still at war. An armistice agreement, rather than a peace treaty, still unsigned by South Korea, ended the 1950-53 Korean War.

Both sides laid claim to the entire country but in the end had to settle for a Demilitarized (frontier) Zone Area (DMZ) spanning latitude 38°. The DMZ is about 2½ miles wide, dividing the land mass of Korea for about 130 miles from the Sea of Japan in the east to the Yellow Sea in the west. The zone is essentially a cease-fire line left over from the war: a no-man's-land of barbed wire, minefields and numerous guard posts zigzagging along the frontier.

The Korean War became the first to be fought by the United Nations, then pro-West under the leadership of the United States. Surprisingly, the Soviet delegation to the UN did not block the action, but this appears to have been an error of judgement rather than intentional.

Korea's traditional enemy was Japan who set up a protectorate over Korea early this century and annexed the whole country in 1910. The Allies called for the restoration of an independent Korea in 1943, and after the war divided the country in two. Soviet Union forces kept control of the north and the United States forces occupied the south. While the Soviets and Americans were about to negotiate details of the unification and independence of North and South, the Cold War started and the two sides became deadlocked. Separate governments were established – the Republic of Korea in the south and the Democratic People's Republic of Korea in the north. In

1948-49 the Soviet and American troops went home.

However, the Soviet Union-backed North Korean army invaded the south on 25 June 1950 with some 200,000 troops in ten infantry divisions, one tank division and an air force division. These forces were too strong for the ill-equipped South Korean army of some 100,000 men, lacking in tanks and heavy artillery as well as combat aeroplanes. Seoul, the South Korean capital, fell within three days. South Korean forces were confined to a territory in the northeast corner of the peninsula 90 miles long and 60 miles wide.

Korea: The 38th Parallel

The United States immediately committed forces in support of South Korea, and President Truman ordered the use of American planes and naval vessels against the North Korean forces as early as 26 June. Four days later American ground troops were committed. The United States feared that no action in Korea would be interpreted as appeasement of Communist aggression elsewhere in the world and was determined that South Korea should not be taken over by a Communist regime. When General MacArthur, the US commanding general of the UN forces in Korea, launched his amphibious attack and landed at Inch on 15 September, the entire war changed abruptly.[1]

A large part of North Korea was taken up by the US and South Korean forces before the Chinese army intervened in October and pushed the UN forces back over the 38th parallel, and the war continued.

The war lasted until 27 July 1953, when a cease-fire agreement was signed at Panmunjom. By that time the fighting had involved both China and the Soviet Union on the North Korean side and on the South Korean side thirteen member nations of the UN contributed armed forces and medical units.

Casualties on both sides were enormous and the war reduced the country to a mass of rubble. Over the forty years since the war numerous skirmishes have taken place along the DMZ, particularly in the 1960s and early 1970s. Since then allegations of infiltration by North Korean agents have dwindled although thousands of truce violations each year along the DMZ have been reported.

The chances for peaceful unification were remote even before 1950, but the war dashed all hope of agreement. Tension in the peninsula remained high and the United States continued to keep troops in the South and China stationed troops in the North.

The impact of the war on North Korea was especially devastating and the population fell from 9.5 million in 1949 to 8.5 million when the war ended. The population of Panmunjom fell from 400,000 to 80,000. A total of half a million North Korean troops were killed.

In January 1968, North Korea seized the USS Pueblo, imprisoned its crew and despatched a commando suicide squad to Seoul in an unsuccessful attempt to assassinate President Park Chung Hee. In November 1968, 120 North Korean commandos were killed or captured in a raid on the South Korean coast and in April 1969 North Korea shot down a US EC-21 reconnaissance plane.

Between 1975 and 1978 three large tunnels were discovered under the DMZ, one of which was 246 feet below ground and near the truce town of Panmunjom. It was presumably to be used as an access tunnel for the infiltration of North Korean agents to offer speedy transfer of troops into the South prior to an invasion.[2]

South Korea countered by constructing a heavily fortified defence line some two to five miles south of the DMZ. South Korea's capital, Seoul, however, although well defended, lies only 25 miles north of this defence zone and is therefore more vulnerable to artillery and missiles from the North. During the 1980s vast North Korean forces were deployed along the DMZ which heightened tension and threat of attack.

Both the Soviet Union and China continued to support North Korea, although in the early 1970s the Soviets stopped sending new weapon systems and advanced technology. However, neither looked for a confrontation with the United States over the Korean peninsula and North Korea continued to demand the evacuation of the 40,000 US troops from South Korea throughout the 1970s and 1980s. The two Koreas were unyielding in their mutual enmity in the 1980s as they had been during the preceding decades.

The policy of both was, and still is, unification, the North advocating an all Korean Commission, or Commonwealth, as they had proposed at the Geneva Conference after the Korean War. However, North Korea are insisting that the establishment of an inter-Korean political formula should be based on parity rather than population since one man-one vote would give South Korea a commanding advantage with twice the population.

When the Berlin Wall crumbled in 1989, South Koreans were amazed and wondered if it could happen to their man-made frontier of barbed wire, mines and tank-traps. But sadly they concluded that it was very unlikely. However, one year later both governments were talking about opening the frontier at Panmunjom for a few days. The first move was made by the North to mark the 45th anniversary of Korea's liberation from Japan. The reason remains a mystery but it is thought that their President Kim Il Sung was blazing with anger when he discovered Mikhail Gorbachev had arranged a private meeting with South Korea's President Roh Tae Woo. He decided, therefore, that he had no choice but to open the channels of communication with the South with which it had no phone, no mail and no air links since the war.

The Prime Minister of each country met in Seoul in September 1990 for two days of discussion and again in October. Although the real power is held by the Presidents, these discussions were more than merely symbolic. They constituted the first occasion on which a meeting had been held at high political level since 1948 and paved the way for a summit meeting of the Presidents in February 1991. It is hoped that this will lead to Korean reunification by the end of the century. Meantime, on 17 September 1991, both countries were independently admitted to the United Nations.[3]

14

THE RADCLIFFE LINE

The Radcliffe Line, which separated India and Pakistan when India was partitioned in 1947, was arguably the most complex frontier award of the century and resulted in massive bloodshed.
Sir Cyril Radcliffe, son of a wealthy sportsman, was a brilliant London barrister who came down from Oxford with a first and an All Soul's Fellowship. He had never been to India and knew very little about the country, but he had been selected by the Prime Minister, Clement Atlee, and Lord Mountbatten, the last Viceroy, to draw a line on the map of India to divide from India the largely Moslem parts of the regions of the Punjab in the west and Bengal in the east. The greatest problem was where the boundary lines dividing these provinces were to fall. On independence day these regions would become West Pakistan and East Pakistan, 1,000 miles apart but administered by the national legislature in Karachi in West Pakistan.
Radcliffe arrived in India on 8 July and was given until 15 August, the Appointed Day for Indian independence, to complete his report. With four High Court judges, he immediately took over as Chairman of the Boundary Commission, which had already had meetings in Calcutta and Lahore without much progress.
The two provinces of the Punjab and Bengal had some 88 million people in about 175,000 square miles, twice the area of the United Kingdom. No matter how he finally drew his line, Radcliffe realised that there would inevitably be anomalies, some of them no doubt serious. He also realised that in the time allotted to him he could not possibly inspect the land

and communities through which his line would be drawn. In his discussions with Mountbatten and later with Pandit Nehru, leader of the Congress Party, and Mohammed Ali Jinnah, Leader of the Muslim League Party, there was no way in which the target date could be put back beyond the Appointed Day.

He set himself up in a bungalow in a quiet suburb of Delhi, and surrounded himself with maps, most of which, although used by the Royal Engineers, were either of insufficient accuracy or of a scale too small for the precision required.

The Punjab was the home for Moslems, Hindus and Sikhs, who had lived reasonably peacefully together under British rule. In the beautiful city of Lahore, in the heart of the Punjab, often deemed at that time 'the Paris of the Orient', there were 500,000 Moslems, 500,000 Hindus and about 100,000 Sikhs. The Punjab was also the home for five of India's six million Sikhs and in nearby Amritsar they prayed in their magnificent Golden Temple.

Radcliffe did visit Lahore to see for himself that, as the Punjab awaited his decision as to where he would draw his boundary, the area seethed with potential strife already simmering under the surface. Like the hurried leap towards independence, he too was being hurried and he knew there would be a penalty to pay. Too little time had been allowed for natural relations to develop among the Indian communities. Nevertheless, Radcliffe had the Boundary Commission Award ready before the Appointed Day. Mountbatten knew that the report would be explosive and therefore preferred to have the independence celebrations first. On the following day Radcliffe's Awards were made public and immediately disputes boiled over. Lahore was given to Pakistan, Amritsar to India, Chittagong Hill Tracts and Sylhet to Pakistan and Calcutta to India.

There were numerous controversies, but a major one concerned the city of Gurdespur, the northern extremity of the Punjab with a small Moslem majority. There, Radcliffe followed the natural boundary line of the Ravi River, leaving the city and Moslem villages around it inside India instead of creating a Pakistani enclave protruding into India. It was a decision which Pakistan would never forget but it gave India access to Kashmir.

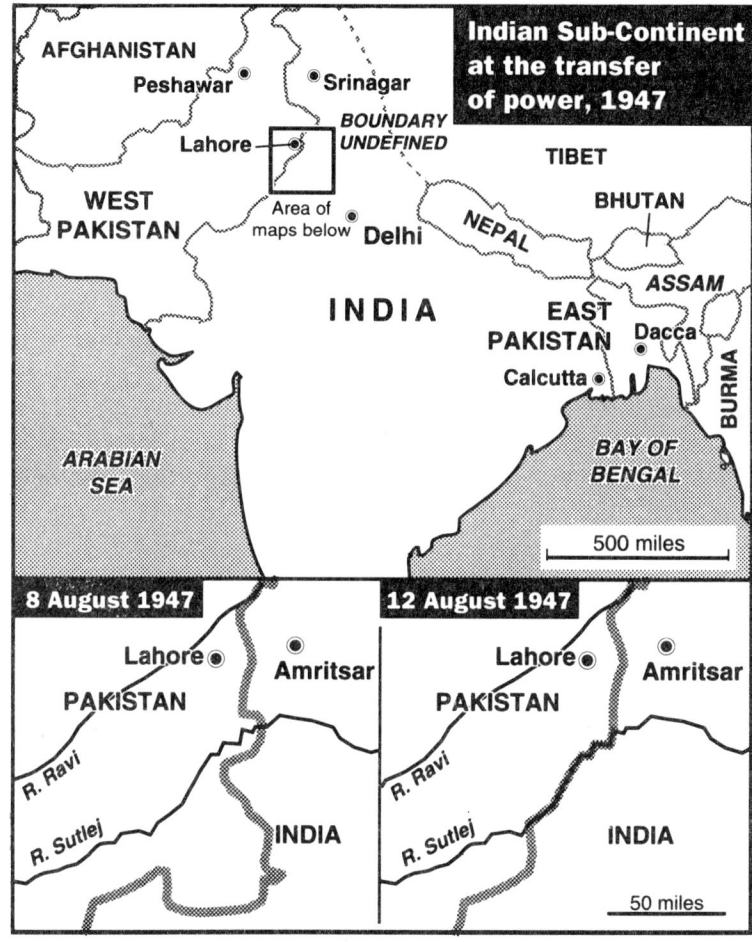

The Radcliffe Line divided villages, separated communities, crossed reservoirs, bisected homes leaving the front door opening on to India and the back door to Pakistan, and all Punjab jails wound up in Pakistan. The Line bisected the lands and peoples of the Sikh community leaving 5 million Sikhs and Hindus in the Pakistan half of the Punjab and over 5 million Moslems in the Indian half. Violence which had been smouldering in early August now erupted into massacres. Trains became death traps as refugees fled to their own side of the new frontier, held by Sikhs on one side and Moslems on the other. Although the worst violence was in the West, where Moslems butchered Hindus and Sikhs, in the East Sikhs butchered Moslems in some of the ugliest massacres witnessed this century.

The precise number of people killed in religious violence during the immediate days after Indian independence is unknown but it has been estimated that as many as 200,000 lost their lives and some 12 million Hindu and Moslem refugees crossed the new frontier in a mass transfer of these two peoples. Over a period of a few years after partition, however, it is generally believed that nearly one million were killed in open conflict and 15 million made homeless.

The Radcliffe Line, no matter where it was drawn, would always have been under dispute, but some of the awards made both parties furious. There was also suspicion on the part of Pakistan that Mountbatten may have amended portions of the Awards in favour of India because Jinnah had refused to appoint him the first Governor General of Pakistan and took the honour himself. A sketch map apparently released by mistake prior to the official Boundary Commission Awards showed the sub-districts of Ferozepur and Zira on the Pakistan side of the proposed frontier, but when the Report was published these regions were included in India.[1]

Kashmir – a Princely State predominantly Moslem in the northwest and bordering the Punjab – has been in dispute with India since the frontier was confirmed in 1947, when Indian and Pakistani troops entered the state and skirmishes took place. Today Pakistan contests about one-third of the state in the west and India the remaining two-thirds.

In August 1965 clashes broke out along the frontier but in September the UN demanded a cease-fire and both sides agreed to withdraw their armies to a prearranged cease-fire line. Clashes also took place in 1965 along the Assam-East Pakistan frontier and in the Ramm of Cutch area along the West Pakistan Gujarat frontier near the Arabian Sea, but the Tashkent agreement of January 1966 ended serious border warfare. An international commission in 1968 awarded 90 per cent of the Ramm to India and the remainder to Pakistan.

After 300 years of British rule, India was rushed to independence, and the Radcliffe Line was decided in just a few weeks. It became a border which was to see more tragedy than any frontier ever conceived before or since. Radcliffe himself left India under a cloud and was so disenchanted that he returned his £2,000 fee to the Government.

Unrest in East Pakistan started soon after independence and in 1969 led to a demand for autonomy.

In 1971 the Pakistan Army moved in to quash the independence movement that was supported by clandestine aid from India and some 10 million Bengali refugees poured across the border into India, creating social, economic and health problems. India signed a friendship treaty with the USSR and quantities of Soviet arms began to enter India. After numerous border incidents, India invaded East Pakistan and in two weeks forced the surrender of the Pakistan Army, taking over 90,000 prisoners. East Pakistan was established as an independent state and renamed Bangladesh. Because of cross-border incursions, leading in 1990 to a death toll of 3,500, India decided, in 1992, to construct a barbed-wire fence along the entire length of its frontier with Pakistan, as it had already done between Jammu, Kashmir and the Punjab.[2] At the beginning of February, more than 700,000 Indian and Pakistani troops faced each other on the frontier of the disputed state of Jammu and Kashmir.[3]

The Radcliffe and McMahon Lines and the disputed frontiers of China-India, China-Commonwealth of Independent States. The 17th and 38th Parallels, Hong Kong, Formosa Strait and the disputed Senkaku Isles. (Part I)

The Radcliffe and McMahon Lines and the disputed frontiers of China-India, China-Commonwealth of Independent States. The 17th and 38th Parallels, Hong Kong, Formosa Strait and the disputed Senkaku Isles. (Part II)

15

THE McMAHON LINE

Sir Henry McMahon, born in Simla in 1802, devoted many years of his life to boundary work and served for many years on the Indian frontiers. In 1911 he became Foreign Secretary of the Government of India and as such took a leading administrative role in designating the frontier line which was to bear his name.

As Chairman of the Sino Tripartite Conference (1913-14) with China and Tibet to determine the northeast frontier of India, he was responsible for successfully drawing up a bilateral agreement between British India and Tibet. The line, still disputed by China (see chapter 18 and map chapter 14), runs along the high crests of the Himalayas from Bhutan to Burma, a distance of some 850 miles. McMahon's surveyors, Bailey, Pritchard, Waterfield and O'Callaghan, had still not finished their survey of the line when the conference started. However, the survey of the entire 850 miles of the tortuous frontier had been completed and the report in McMahon's hands before the conference finished in July 1914.[1] Britain was the greatest beneficiary of the Sino talks, for McMahon had gained some 50,000 square miles of Himalayan territory for British India.[2] China refused to sign the agreement on the proposed line on the grounds that Tibet was subordinate to China and had no authority to make treaties. The Chinese maintained this position until the frontier controversy with India led to the Sino-Indian War (Oct-Nov 1962). China has not subsequently pressed its claim to Indian territory by force, and the McMahon Line still forms the Sino-Indian frontier.

Sir Henry McMahon's predecessor as Foreign Secretary of

the Government of India was Sir Mortimer Durand and he too was involved in boundary work. It was Sir Mortimer who established the India-Afghanistan frontier by negotiation with the Afghan armies, known since then as the Durand Line.[3]

16

THE CURZON LINE

Poland's eastern frontier with the Soviet Union is based on the Curzon Line – an ethnically-defined frontier first proposed during the Russian-Polish War of 1919-20 by the British Foreign Secretary, Lord Curzon. After the Second World War the Curzon Line, which had never really been proposed as a permanent border, was revived by the Soviet Union when it claimed all the territory east of the line and occupied the area in accordance with the German-Soviet Non-aggression Pact of 1939. After the German's retreat in 1944, the Soviet Union occupied all of Poland's territory. At the Yalta Conference in February 1945 the US and UK agreed to Soviet demands on Poland and recognised the Curzon Line as the Soviet-Polish border. The Soviet-Polish treaty of August 1945 officially designated a line almost identical to the Curzon Line as their mutual frontier.[1] Historically, the line was originally drawn in 1919 by a commission on Polish affairs of the Paris Supreme Council to mark the eastern limit of indisputable Polish territory. The proposal became associated with Lord Curzon a year later when it was put before the two parties in an attempt to bring hostilities to an end.[2]

Minor territorial adjustments in 1945 moved Poland's physical centre westwards and involved a considerable movement of the population. Clearly, the Atlantic Charter was not recognized in the delineation of Poland's frontiers (see Appendix). Some 3 million people were removed from their homes in the east part of the country and resettled in the newly acquired western lands from which some 2.5 million Germans were in turn removed between 1946 and 1949 (see chapter 9).[3] Because of the war and frontier changes, Poland's population fell from 35 million in 1939 to 25 million in 1950. In 1939 about 30 per cent of the population was 96 per cent ethnic Polish, of whom 90 per cent were Roman Catholics.

The Curzon Line (1921)

The movement of frontiers, of which the Curzon Line was just one example, and the consequent vast transformations of territory in multi-ethnic Poland over the last 200 years, has resulted in distressing social disruption. Because of frontier changes it was possible for a Pole to have been born and brought up in Austria, have married in Austria, have lived and worked in Poland, been killed in Germany and buried in the Soviet Union – all without moving from the same house, in the same street, in the same town.

17

CHINA - SOVIET UNION FRONTIER DISPUTES

China's frontiers of some 12,500 miles are shared with Afghanistan, Pakistan, Bhutan, Burma, India, Laos, Mongolia, Nepal, North Korea, Vietnam, Sikkin, and the Soviet Union. There are 8,500 miles of coastline and some 5,000 offshore islands. The frontiers are in dispute at a number of points, and the 4,300 mile frontier with the Soviet Union has been a source of conflict since the mid-nineteenth century when China lost substantial territory to tsarist Russia (see map, chapter 14).[1]

Maps published in China today show substantial areas of Soviet territory as part of the People's Republic of China. However, this claim is rejected by the Soviet Union.

In the west, China claims part of the 16,000 square mile Pamir area, a region of mountain peaks and glacial valleys where the frontiers of Afghanistan, the Soviet Union and China meet in central Asia. North and east of the Pamir region, some sections of the border are imperfectly demarcated and therefore in dispute. In the north-east, frontier disputes often produce a tense situation in remote regions of Nei Monggol Autonomous Region (Inner Mongolia) and Heilongjiang Province along sections of the Rivers Argun, Amur and Ussuri. In the 1960s, troops from each side were massed along the frontier and clashes occurred from time to time, continuing into the 1970s.

In May 1978, Soviet troops in river gunboats and helicopters, crossed the Ussuri River and invaded Chinese territory for a short period. Fortunately diplomacy recovered the situation and a major crisis was avoided. Nevertheless, during the early 1980s the Soviet Union maintained up to a quarter of their ground and tactical air forces along the Chinese frontier. With the Chinese military build-up also increasing, provocations frequently occurred as the two sides faced each other menacingly across the frontier.

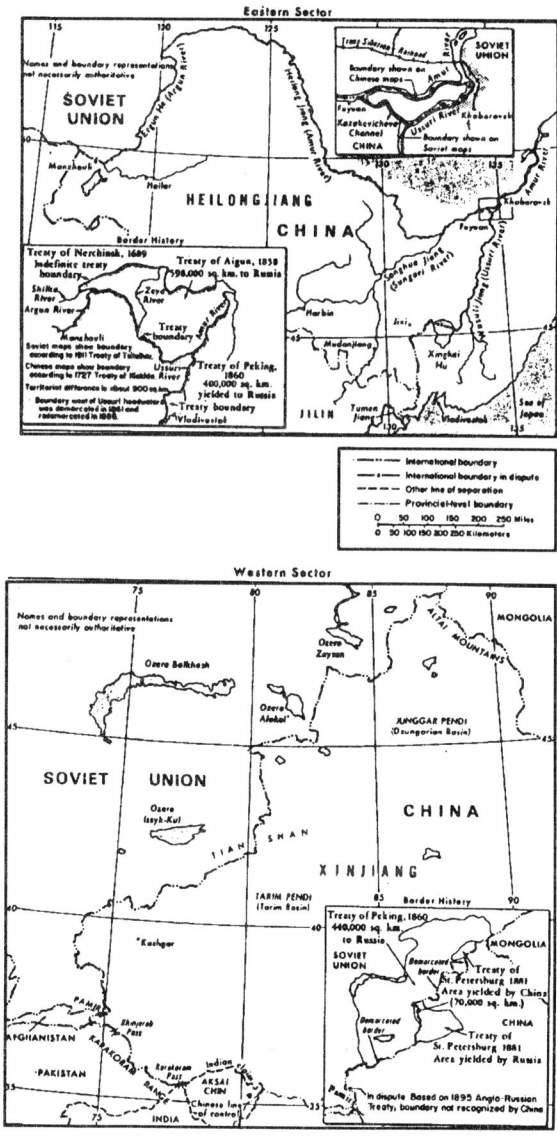

China-CIS frontiers

The strengths of each side along the frontier today are unknown. It is believed that before 1985 the Soviet Union maintained by far the strongest military force with six armoured and thirty-eight mechanized infantry divisions supported by over 2,000 combat aircraft. China, for its part, deployed eight divisions, with additional divisions available as reinforcements as necessary. Despite its greater strength in manpower military experts agreed that the Chinese forces were on the whole deficient in fire-power. However, they also concluded that although a Soviet invasion would initially have gained some valuable Chinese territory, China would in all probability have stemmed the invasion and called up their reinforcements before the Soviet army reached Peking.

Today the frontier is quiet, due in no small measure to the coming in 1985 of glasnost and peristroika with Mikhail Gorbachev and Eduard Shevardnadze. Discussions by Peking and Moscow on their disputed frontier were virtually completed in April 1991 and agreement apparently reached on over 90 per cent of the border, leaving only eight sections where agreement is still needed.[2] With the collapse of the Soviet Union, however, new frontier problems will inevitably arise and peoples in the Moslem region of Xinjiang in North West China may wish to forge closer links with the independent states of Kirghizia, Tadzhikistan and Kazakhstan, The frontier separating the peoples of Inner Mongolia and Mongolia may also come under pressure as well as the unstable China-Tibet frontier.

Building the Berlin Wall in August 1961.

Soviet occupation troops enter Wenceslas Square in Prague on August 21, 1968.

Dozens of Soviet tanks guard the street intersection which leads to the Danube Bridge in Budapest, November 4, 1956.

Adolf Hitler drives into Vienna on March 14, 1938 to take possession of the Austrian capital while enormous crowds give him a rousing reception.

A group of Neo-Nazis give the Nazi salute at the Oder-Neisse border at Frankfurt/Oder, April 8, 1991, on the opening of the frontier between Germany and Poland.

West Berliners crowd Potsdamer Platz on November 12, 1989 to watch the East Germans pulling down segments of the Berlin Wall.

Romanian demonstrators in Tirgu Mures beat up a man who belongs to the 40 per cent Hungarian minority group in Tirgu Mures, March 22, 1990.

Yugoslav army tanks pass a signpost in Maribor indicating directions to the border between Slovenia and Austria, June 27, 1991.

Tanks of the Federal Yugoslavian army remove vehicles built up as a blockade near the Yugoslavian-Austrian frontier near Spielfeld, June 27, 1991.

Lithuanians make an attempt to aid a protester who lies in front of a Soviet tank after Soviet tanks were used in an assault on the radio-television station in Vilnius.

East Berliners passing through Checkpoint Charlie to visit the West, many for the first time, November 1989.

Berliners on top of the Berlin Wall welcoming East Germans through the wall into West Berlin at Potsdamer Platz, November 12, 1989.

Yugoslav Federal army guardsmen display a Croatian flag which they captured in Vukovar on November 18, 1991.

The end of the International Patrol in Vienna. Four soldiers of the Occupying Powers shake hands outside the headquarters of the Allied High Commission in Vienna. When the patrol ended, four soldiers from the four countries, Britain, France, the Soviet Union and the United States had patrolled the Austrian capital for ten years (1945-55). They became better known as 'Four Men in a Jeep'.

The signing of the Peace Treaty of Versailles in the Hall of Mirrors in the Palace of Versailles, June 28, 1919.

Above right: The signing of the Treaty of St. Germain-en-Laye (the Austrian Treaty) in the Palace of St. Germain in the western outskirts of Paris, September 10, 1919.

Police attack demonstrators in Trieste, March 22, 1952.

Turkish armed forces in Cyprus. After the Turkish forces invaded Cyprus from Kyrenia, they controlled the road from Kyrenia to Nicosia, July 1974.

Removing a barricade on the 'Green Line' in Beirut under the supervision of the security forces.

The Oder-Neisse border. The Polish town of Görlitz was cut into the Polish and German parts by the River Neisse. The picture shows the River Neisse and Polish occupied part of Görlitz.

People of Niedergardern, formerly West Germany serenade their friends and relatives living on the other side of the frontier formed by a barbed wire fence in Kirchgadorn. The Communist police kept the people of Kirchgadorn in their houses, November 6, 1961.

A primitive Indian fort on a ledge facing the Chinese troops in the Ladekh frontier region, October 1962.

The monument marks where the old frontiers of Poland, Danzig and East Prussia met in accordance with the Treaty of Versailles, July 3, 1939.

British soldiers watch as a section of the Berlin Wall is being built November 22, 1961.

India and Pakistan go to war over the disputed territory of Kashmir. The picture shows refugees escaping from Kashmir September 6, 1965.

Some four years after the Second World War the Netherlands Government put into force its claims for minor rectification along the Dutch-German frontier as agreed by the Six Power Committee in Paris in 1949. The area involved was some 70 square kilometres and 9000 people. The photograph shows a party of civilians and Netherlands troops and police marking the new frontier on April 24, 1949.

Sino-Soviet frontier clashes over the disputed islands in the Ussuri River took place at regular intervals in the late sixties and early seventies and although these conflicts have ceased, the dispute over the frontier has never been resolved. The photograph, taken in March 1969, shows Chinese troops remonstrating with Soviet troops on the frontier.

Tirgu Mures, March 23, 1990. Soldiers from the Romanian crack parachute regiment maintain peace after a clash between Romanians and the Hungarian ethnic minority when six people were killed.

An Israeli Defence Forces armoured personnel carrier crosses into Israel after returning from a military operation in Southern Lebanon including attacks on the villages of Yatar and Kafra, February 21, 1992.

18

CHINA - INDIA FRONTIER DISPUTES

On the western end of China's frontier with India, formed by the mountain barrier of the Himalayas, a major dispute focuses on the Aksai Chin area of northeast Jammu and Kashmir. The region is under Chinese control but claimed by India. Further east, China has never recognised the present Indian frontier with Tibet, drawn by Sir Henry McMahon (see chapter 15) in 1914, and invaded India in 1962 for a brief spell before withdrawing. In this incursion in both Ladakh and a region north of the Brahmaputra river India suffered inglorious defeat. In June 1980, after 20 years of mutual respect, China tried to settle the border dispute by proposing that India cede the Aksai Chin region in Kashmir to China, in return for China's recognition of the McMahon Line (see map, chapter 14).

In 1988, opposing troops nearly started a shooting conflict in the Sundarong Chin Valley in Arunchal Pradesh when India accused China of secretly fortifying the valley and China accused India of attempting to nibble at Chinese territory.

In total, some one thousand miles of Chinese-Indian frontier and some 50,000 square miles of disputed territory are under dispute. Relations between the two countries started to deteriorate as a result of a series of revolts against Chinese rule after their 1950 invasion of Tibet, culminating on 17 March 1959 in the rising in Lhasa which was suppressed by China. The Dalai Lama and hundreds of Tibetan refugees fled to India and were granted political asylum, much to the anger of China who accused India of having assisted, if not encouraged, the rebels.[1] In this dispute the Soviet Union gave moral support to India as a result of growing tension between Moscow and Peking. Chinese policy on the frontier, which has never wavered, was clearly stated by Chou-En-lai at a Press Conference in New Delhi on 30 April 1960 when, in response to a question on the disputed Sino-Indian frontier, he said:[2]

> There are disputes both with regard to the eastern sector and the western sector. As regards the middle sector, the dispute is comparatively small. Regarding the eastern sector: the boundary line which appears on our maps is to the south of the boundary line on Indian maps. The area included in India on Indian maps had long been under Chinese administrative jurisdiction. Since its independence, India has gradually moved forward up to the line delineated on its present maps. The Indian Government asks us to recognise this line which it sometimes even openly said is the McMahon Line. We absolutely cannot recognise this line, because it was illegally delineated through an exchange of secret notes by British imperialism with the Tibetan local authorities of China, and the successive Chinese Governments have never recognised it. Nevertheless, pending a settlement of the Sino-Indian boundary question, we are willing to maintain the present state and will not cross this line; in negotiations on the Boundary question, too, we have not put forward territorial claims as pre-conditions. Since we have adopted such an attitude of understanding and conciliation, it appears that comparatively less time has been spent on discussions of the eastern sector of the boundary.
>
> With regard to the western sector; the way of delineation of the boundary on Chinese maps is different from that on Indian maps. Despite small discrepancies which exist in the delineations of this sector on past Chinese maps, these maps are in the main consistent. The Indian maps, however, have changed many times. China has always exercised

administrative jurisdiction in accordance with the line on Chinese maps, that is, the line which runs from the Karakoram pass southeastward roughly along the watershed of Karakoram Mountain to the Kongka Pass, then turns southward from the Kongka Pass and extends to the vicinity of the Pare river. The border area to the north and east of this line has historically been under the jurisdiction of China. The greater part of it, including the Aksai Chin area, is under the jurisdiction of Sinkiang of China, and the smaller part under the jurisdiction of Tibet of China. We have many historical documents and materials to prove this historical administrative jurisdiction. Since the founding of New China, it has always exercised jurisdiction in this area as the main communication artery linking southern Sinkiang and the Ari area of Tibet. With regard to this area, the delineation of the boundary on Indian maps before the middle of the nineteenth century was approximate to that on Chinese maps. During the period from 1865 to 1943, the more important maps of India were quite vague with regard to the delineation of this sector of the boundary. The official Indian map of 1950 used colour shades to indicate an outline of this sector of the boundary as is now advocated by India. Nevertheless, the map still marked the area as undelimited. Finally, in 1954, the line, just like the eastern sector of the boundary, became as if it had been formally delineated as shown on the map you now see in Indian newspapers. Therefore, even the changes of the Indian maps during the past one hundred years and more can also fully prove that the boundary in this area is undelimited. We have asked the Indian Government to adopt an attitude towards this area similar to the attitude of the Chinese Government towards the area of the eastern sector, that is, it may keep its own stand, while agreeing to conduct negotiations and not to cross the line of

China's administrative jurisdiction as shown on Chinese maps. The Indian Government has not entirely agreed to this. Therefore, there exists a relatively bigger dispute and the two Prime Ministers have spent a particularly long period of time on discussions in this connection. With regard to the middle sector there are also disputes but they are questions concerning individual places.

There were no further negotiations on the frontier issue for over thirty years until December 1991, when Prime Minister Li Peng met his Indian counterpart, Narashima Rao, in New Delhi. The frontier issue was not raised at this meeting, and nor did India receive any support on the Kashmir problem. China, however, got India to reaffirm that it considers Tibet an autonomous region of China with the Dalai Lama as its spiritual head only.

19

JAPAN - SOVIET UNION ISLANDS' DISPUTE

Because of a continuing territorial dispute, no peace treaty formally ending the Second World War has been signed between Japan and the Soviet Union. The dispute is over four of the Kurile Islands: Etorofu and Kunashiri, and the smaller Shikotan and Habomai island group, northeast of Hokkaido. These islands were occupied by the Soviet Union in the final days of the Pacific war in return for her participation in the war against Japan, and Japan insists that they must be returned as a condition for signing a peace treaty.

The Kurile Islands

The four northern islands in question are separated by narrow straits and form a natural entity extending along a northeast-southwest axis. In 1947 the United States endeavoured to sign a peace treaty with Japan. It was opposed by the Soviet Union, and it was not until 1951 that a treaty was formally signed by the US and Japan in San Francisco ending the Second World War. The treaty, however, confirmed the loss of all former Japanese overseas possessions including the Kurile Islands and Southern Sakhalin, both of which had been under Soviet occupation since the end of the war. In order to keep the issue alive, Japan has celebrated 'Northern Territories Day' on 7 February every year since 1980, and it has been reported in the Japanese press that Japan was prepared to offer up to $28 billion in aid to the Soviet Union in return for the islands.[1] However, during President Gorbachev's four-day visit to Japan in April 1991, talks on the islands' issue with Japan's Prime Minister Toshiki Kaifu collapsed.[2]

Another long-standing territorial dispute over a tiny chain of islands in the East China Sea between Japan, China and Taiwan, flared up in 1990. The islands, known as the Senkaku chain, consist of five, tiny, uninhabited rock islands and three reefs, 100 miles north east of Taiwan.[3] Japan has asserted sovereignty over the islands since they were returned by the United States along with Okinawa to Japan in 1971. However, Taiwan and China are challenging Japan's claim. Scientists have reported that there may be vast oil reserves in the area, but Japan resisted the temptation to start drilling in view of the sensitivity of Taipei and Peking. The dispute came to a head in October, when Japanese coastguard vessels and helicopters turned back Taiwan athletes seeking to land on one of the islands to plant an Olympic flag as a symbol of Taipei's claim of sovereignty (see map, chapter 14).

20

THE FORMOSA STRAIT DISPUTED FRONTIER

The island province of Taiwan (formerly Formosa), including the sixty-four Pescadores (Penghus) Islands and fourteen other islands plus Quemoy and Matsu, came under mainland control after a period of Dutch rule between 1620 and 1662. It was administered by Japan from 1895 until 1945. Towards the end of the war against the Chinese Communist regime, the nationalist leader General Chiang Kai-Shek, with his 50,000 troops and two million Kuointang (Guomindang) followers, fled from the mainland to set up the Nationalist government in Taiwan in 1949. The Formosa Strait, about 100 miles across, became the maritime frontier between the two countries but the Peoples Republic of China refused to accept Taiwan's existence and has always claimed the island as its 27th Province (see map, chapter 14).

Mainly because Taiwan spoke for all China at the United Nations, it took over twenty years for a two-thirds majority in the UN to support a motion for the People's Republic to take up membership. When it did in 1971, Taiwan was expelled and China became the fifth permanent member of the United Nations, joining Britain, France, the United States and the USSR.[1]

In December 1990, Taiwan declared that it would finally end its state of war with the Peoples Republic of China, and so rescind a forty-two year-old emergency declaration issued during the civil war and complete a process of constitutional reform. Such reform will set the stage for the eventual reunification of Taiwan with mainland China, and the Formosa Strait contiguous frontier will disappear for ever.

THE DISPUTED TERRITORY OF ANTARCTICA

Antarctica, a continent with a 15 million years old ice cap amounting to some 10 per cent of the Earth's land mass, has seven nations pressing territorial claims but is owned by no one. The claiming nations are Argentina, Australia, Britain, Chile, France, New Zealand and Norway. The borders of the British, Chilean and Argentine claims overlap, and Australia, Chile and Argentina have been the most active in keeping their claims alive.

Little exploration of Antarctica was carried out until the 19th century, and although Sir Ernest Shackleton got within 112 miles of the South Pole in 1909, it was not until 14 December 1911 that Roald Amundsen and four of his Norwegian countrymen became the first to reach the Pole. Robert Falcon Scott and his team of four arrived just five weeks later on 17 January 1912; all died on the fatal return journey.

However, it was in 1820 that three explorers laid claim to discovering Antarctica. They were Edward Bransfield, UK who charted Trinity Island just off the Antarctic Peninsula; Nathaniel Brown Palmer, US who sailed the west coast of the Peninsula, and FS von Bellingshausen, Russia, who sighted what may have been the mainland during his circumnavigation. In 1821 John Davis, US, sent sealers ashore at Hughes Bay to claim the first landing on the continent of Antarctica.[1]

The thirst for oil, gas and minerals has inspired nations to keep the Antarctic under review, but these natural resources, if available, are locked under a gigantic sheet of moving ice with an average thickness of 1¼ miles (2km) and a maximum thickness of nearly 3 miles (5 km). The average elevation of

Antarctica is about 6,000 ft (1,830 m), with a maximum of 14,271 ft (4,351 m). Darkness prevails for 6 months of the year and temperatures drop to -90° C (-129° F). It has an area of some 5.4 million square miles (14 million square kilometres), equal to the size of the US and Europe together. Only a small part has so far been explored. Mineral finds, including coal, copper, silver, gold, manganese, cobalt and platinum, are reported to be significant. In addition, three-quarters of the world's fresh water is locked in the ice of the Antarctic and dry nations have looked upon icebergs the size of Luxembourg with envy.

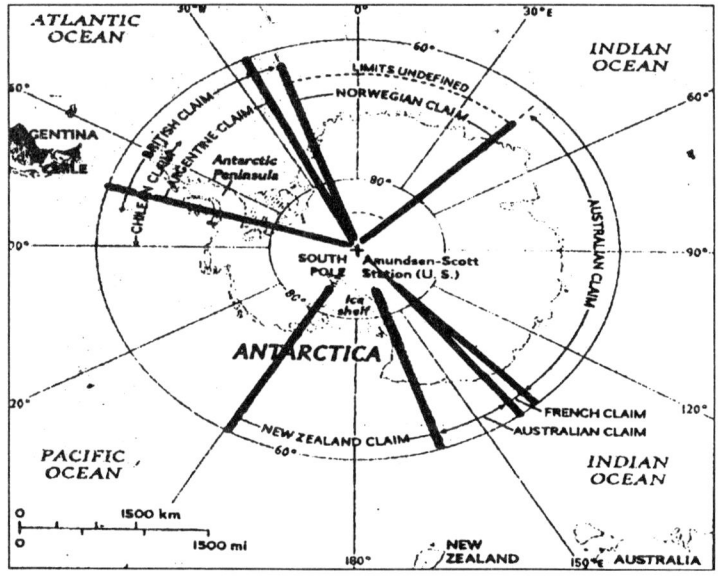

Antarctica: Territorial Claims

In view of the importance of the continent and the international politics involved, the Antarctic Treaty was signed in 1959 by twelve scientifically active nations – Argentina, Australia, Belgium, Chile, France, Japan, New Zealand, Norway, South Africa, the Soviet Union, the United Kingdom and the United States. Since then considerable scientific research has been undertaken on the continent and over 3,000 permanent residents operate some fifty-seven scientific stations, twenty-three of them on the Peninsula. These are controlled by eighteen countries. The terms of the treaty are now accepted by a further twenty-two nations but the treaty does not interfere with the historical territorial claims under dispute.

Meantime, the 1988 Convention on the Regulation of Antarctic Mineral Resource Activities (CRAMRA) agreement, which took the nineteen participating countries six years to negotiate, has fallen apart.[2] This treaty would allow mineral extraction under strict conditions, and apparently safeguard the environment and ecology. A petition supporting a 'world wilderness park' raised by the World Wide Fund for Nature, Greenpeace and the National Federation of Women's Institutes, received half a million signatures. Also, Mr Robert Sevan, the Antarctic explorer, and Lady Scott, widow of naturalist Sir Peter Scott (son of Robert Falcon Scott), sent a written plea to the Prime Minister, Margaret Thatcher. In November and December 1990, a meeting of the thirty-nine nations to the 1961 Antarctic Treaty held in Vina del Mar, Chile, to resolve the problem ended in a stalemate on the central issue of mining rights. Australia, France and New Zealand headed a group of ten countries which continue to argue for a permanent total ban on future mining in the region. However, a second group, including Britain, the Netherlands, the Soviet Union, the United States and South Africa, wanted a convention ratified which would allow mining within each other's disputed frontiers. The outcome of the eighteen day meeting was simply an agreement to continue talking, and a further meeting held in Spain in April of the following year agreed on a fifty year ban on exploitation of mineral resources.[3]

22

GIBRALTAR

The fortress of Gibraltar is connected to the Spanish mainland by a road leading to the frontier at the town of La Linea. Its position has great strategic importance to NATO as it had for the Allies during two World Wars and during the Cold War.
 The Rock was occupied by the Moors from North Africa from 711 to 1309, and again from 1333 until 1462. Spain occupied the fortress between these periods and subsequently, until the War of Spanish Succession in 1702 when Britain was allied with the Netherlands and Austria against France. The main objective of the war was to place Archduke Charles of Austria on the throne of Spain instead of Phillip V who was supported by France.
 In 1704 the British under Sir George Rooke decided to attack Gibraltar and use the fortress as a base during the war, since Britain had previously given up the port of Tangier which it had acquired in 1662 from Portugal. After a siege of three days the Rock was captured in the name of Archduke Charles, who became Charles III of Spain. The Rock passed to Britain by the Treaty of Utrecht (1713). Spain tried unsuccessfully, with French help, to regain possession of the fortress, but renounced it's claim in 1729 in favour of its South American possessions.[1] In 1779, during the American War of Independence, the Great Siege of Gibraltar by the Spanish and French began. It lasted three years but ended in defeat for Spain once again and the Treaty of Versailles (1783) confirmed British possession.
 Since then, Spanish claims to the Rock have never ceased,

but while Spain claims that a foreign enclave on its coast is not acceptable, it takes the opposite view with respect to its possession of Ceuta and Melilla on the North African coast, the last remaining territories in Africa still ruled by a European state.

Gibraltar

In 1966 the United Nations, acting on the recommendations of its Committee on Decolonisation, passed a resolution calling on Britain to expedite the decolonisation of Gibraltar. In 1967 Britain decided to test the Gibraltarians' reaction and held a referendum. The people of Gibraltar were asked to say which of the following alternatives would best serve their interests:[2]

> A. To pass under Spanish sovereignty in accordance with the terms proposed by the Spanish Government to Her Majesty's Government (the rescission of the Treaty of Utrecht and the return of Gibraltar),

or B.

> Voluntarily to retain their link with Britain with democratic local institutions and with Britain retaining its present responsibilities.

The result was forty-four votes for A and 12,138 votes for B, a 99.6 per cent majority in favour of remaining with the United Kingdom. However, the United Nations condemned the referendum and invited Britain to decolonise Gibraltar in accordance with paragraph 6 of Resolution 1514 (xv) which reads:[3]

> Any attempt aimed at the partial or total disruption of the national unity and territorial integrity of a country is incompatible with the purposes and principles of the Charter of the United Nations.

But paragraph 2 reads:

> 2. All peoples have the right to self-determination; by virtue of that right they freely determine their political status and freely pursue their economic, social and cultural development.

The UN made no reference to paragraph 2. Inconclusive talks between Britain and Spain have continued over the years since 1967 but the frontier remains at La Linea.

HONG KONG

The crown colony of Hong Kong (Hiang Kians) comprises the island of Hong Kong, Stonecutters' Island, Kowloon peninsula, and the New Territories (total area 400 square miles). The island of Hong Kong was ceded to Britain in perpetuity, by the Treaty of Nanking (1842) at the end of the Opium Wars, and in 1860 the southern part of the peninsula of Kowloon and Stonecutters' Island were ceded by the Convention of Peking.[1] Further expansion was found to be desirable because of western rivalry in China involving Russia, France and Germany, and in 1898 the British government obtained a 99-year lease from China of the New Territories, including 236 islands, for the sum of £500. The new frontier would be the Shum Chan River between Deep Bay and Sha Tau Kok.[2]

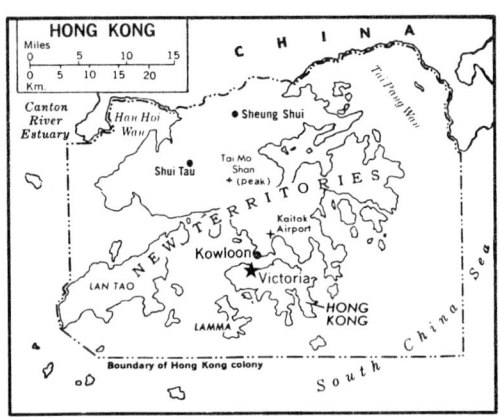

Hong Kong

The Chinese Government have taken the view that the whole of Hong Kong is Chinese territory and that the treaties are unequal ones left over from history. Since the new territories make up some 92 per cent of the total area of Hong Kong, the remaining 8 per cent would not be viable, especially as the former contains most of the territory's agriculture and industry, its power stations, airport and container port. It has long been accepted, therefore, that the whole of Hong Kong will return to China.[3]

Hong Kong was occupied by Japan in 1941 and remained under Japanese rule until August 1945. The colony possesses an excellent natural harbour, the only deep-sea anchorage between Shanghai and Southeast Asia.

On acquiring Hong Kong in 1841, Queen Victoria and Prince Albert may have been amused, but the Foreign Secretary, Lord Palmerston, considered it a white elephant - 'A barren island with hardly a house upon it'. It was clear to him that Britain's Superintendent of Trade in China Captain Charles Elliot, who was responsible for the deal, had made a serious blunder and he had him replaced! Today, with its twin cities of Victoria and Kowloon and nearly 6 million people and four stock exchanges, Hong Kong is the world's third largest financial centre and its eleventh largest trading economy, second only to Japan in East Asia. It boasts more Rolls Royces per acre than any other place on earth.

By a Sino-British treaty signed by both parties – but not by Hong Kong – registered at the United Nations, the colony will pass to the Peoples' Republic of China in 1997, according to the 99-year lease. The treaty provides for China to retain the structure of Britain's capitalist system for fifty years thereafter. But at midnight on 30 June 1997, the 150 year-old frontier between China and Hong Kong will disappear forever.

24

NORTHERN IRELAND

The treaty signed on 6 December 1921 between Britain and the Irish Free State provided that, if the Parliament of Northern Ireland should vote not to be included in the Free State, a commission of three (one member from the Free State, one from Northern Ireland and one from Britain) should determine the frontier between the two countries 'in accordance with the wishes of the inhabitants so far as may be compatible with economic and geographic conditions'.

On 7 December 1922 the Parliament of Northern Ireland claimed that the Government of Ireland Act of 1920 definitely included in Northern Ireland the counties of Antrim, Armagh, Down, Fermanagh, Londonderry and Tyrone and the Boroughs of Belfast and Londonderry, and that the commission was only competent to make minor frontier readjustments justified by local interests. The commission made investigations on the spot regarding the wishes of the inhabitants along the frontier, but the Northern Ireland commissioner refused to attend the investigation, and later the Free State commissioner also withdrew. The powers of the commission were revoked and the frontier left unchanged, the Free State surrendering its position in return for release from liability to contribute towards the service of British debt and war pensions.

The delineated frontier left many glaring anomalies. In the south the line follows rivers and streams or hedges; in the west there are few cross-border roads; in the east the border crosses many roads, lanes and footpaths and people often ignore the frontier and cross-border traffic is common and legitimate. The Irish Republican Army (IRA) operates across the border at will, and the nature of the frontier makes it difficult strategically for the security patrols.[1]

Northern Ireland's history is part of the history of Ireland, but in the 12th century the Pope gave all Ireland to the English Crown as a papal fief. In 1171, Henry II of England was acknowledged 'Lord of Ireland', but local sectional rule continued for centuries and English rule was not absolute until the 17th century.

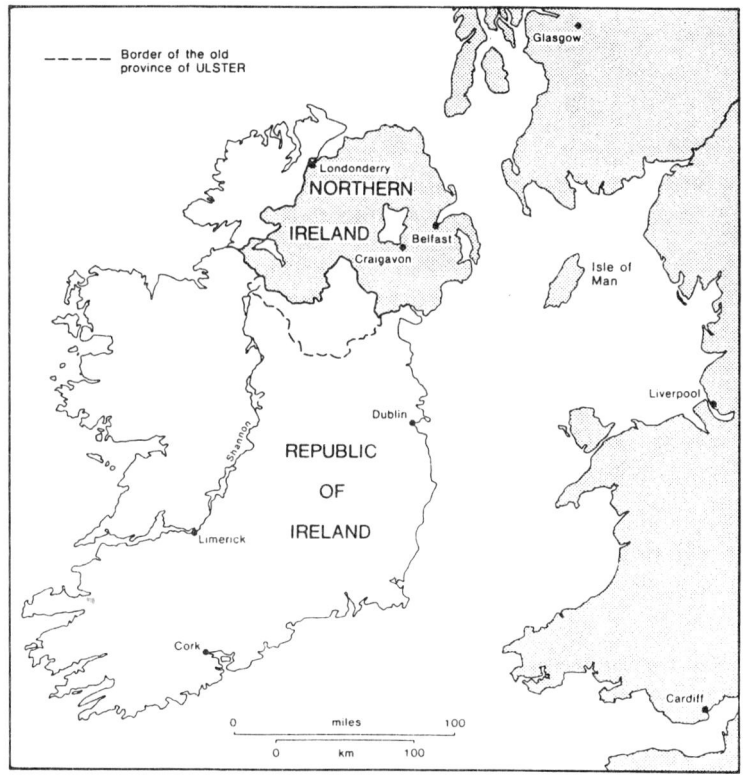

By the Act of Union of 1800, Ireland became part of the United Kingdom. The population grew to 8.5 million, but the great potato famine of 1846-48 took many lives and hundreds of thousands emigrated to the United States.

By 1921 the population had fallen to just over four million. The demands of 'home-rule for Ireland' were growing just before the First World War, and resulted in the Easter Rebellion in Dublin on 24-29 April 1916, in which the Irish Nationalists unsuccessfully tried to throw off British rule. Guerilla warfare against British forces followed the proclamation of a republic by the rebels in 1919.

The treaty of 1921 established the Irish Free State as a dominion, but in 1949 all ties with Britain were broken when the Free State became the Republic of Ireland (Eire). Although the Republic's political system closely resembles that of its former conqueror, Irish democracy differs from the Westminster model and has a written constitution adopted in 1937. Article 2 of this constitution demands the Unification of Ireland:

> 'The national territory consists of the whole island of Ireland, its islands and territorial seas'.

Although the British government in the Second World War was prepared to invade and occupy the Republic if it seemed possible that Britain's sea lanes could be threatened, the two countries recognised and accepted the border as sacrosanct. A United Ireland, however, came close to reality on two separate occasions. The first was when Winston Churchill offered Eamon de Valera, Irish Prime Minister, a United Ireland early in the Second World War if Ireland would join the Allies against Germany. A second occasion offered itself in 1958, when, in a secret meeting with Lord Home, British Foreign Secretary, de Valera offered to rejoin the British Commonwealth in return for a United Ireland. Nothing came of either proposal. The outlawed IRA increased its terrorist efforts in the 1960s to bring the North into the Republic and have continued these activities ever since. Despite public sympathy for the unification of Ireland, the Dublin government deals rigorously with IRA guerillas caught inside its borders. Since 1970, however, IRA terrorists have taken 3,000 lives in Northern Ireland.

A referendum held on 8 March 1973 produced the following result: 591,820 votes for Ulster to remain in the United Kingdom with only 6,463 against, or a 99 per cent majority. A succession of Northern Ireland Prime Ministers pressed reform programmes but failed to satisfy extremists on either side. Britain suspended the Northern Ireland Parliament in 1972 and imposed direct rule from Westminster. A coalition government was formed in 1973 when moderates won election to a new one-house Assembly, but a Protestant general strike overthrew the government in 1974 and direct rule was resumed. In 1985 the Hillsborough Agreement gave the Republic a voice in the governing of Northern Ireland. This was strongly opposed by Ulster loyalists.

In May 1991, after five major political attempts over a period of 21 years to bring peace to Northern Ireland, a sixth and cautiously optimistic attempt involving all four political parties began in Belfast. A crucial factor in the success of the talks would be Dublin's willingness to amend the Irish constitution and remove its territorial claim on Ulster.[2]

AFRICA'S DISPUTED FRONTIERS

The frontiers of the forty-six countries of Africa were delineated by lines drawn across the vast continent by the former colonial powers. In some cases they were haphazardly demarcated, in others they have stood the test of time. Many are in dispute.

Sudan

Sudan was known as Anglo-Egyptian Sudan between 1898 and 1955, and independence from Britain and Egypt was declared in 1956. The country is divided into its twelve northern provinces, which are predominantly Arab-Moslem and its three southern provinces, mainly Negro and Christian-Pagan. Different factions have been at conflict since 1964, but by a 1972 peace agreement the southern provinces won autonomy. However, the situation is still unstable. In addition, Sudan's frontiers with Chad and the Central African Republic are by no means accepted either by the southern provinces or its neighbours. This is especially the case with respect to its conflict with Chad over the Ouaddai region.[1,2]

Ethiopia

Black Africa's oldest state, Ethiopia (formerly Abyssinia), can trace 2,000 years of recorded history. However, the diffuse realm, in which seventy languages are spoken, has suffered a tragic existence over the last fifty years. Thirty of those years have seen a brutal civil war and three catastrophic droughts. The civil war finally ended in 1991 in a victory for the anti-government front consisting of the People's

Revolutionary Democratic Front (PRDF) and the People's Liberation Front (PLF). The former demand a broad based transitional administration leading to democratic elections, and the latter demand independence for Eritrea.[3]

A frontier dispute in the Kassala-Gallabat area between Ethiopia and Sudan, which also concerns Eritrea, has now very little likelihood of being settled amicably. Another frontier dispute with Somalia concerns the Ogaden region, at present in Ethopia but claimed by Somalia although there is no agreed delineation of the whole frontier between the two countries. These disputes await the outcome of the peace conference.

Somalia

In 1920 Somalia became a joint British and Italian protectorate. After 1941 the British took over the rule of the entire country, but Italy returned in 1950 to serve as a UN trustee in its former sector. The British granted independence to its former sector in 1960, and both sectors joined to become the Republic of Somalia. When Britain granted the northern frontier district of Kenya, an area mainly Somalian populated, to the Republic of Kenya in 1963, Somalia broke off diplomatic relations with its former protector.[4]

In 1977 Somalia openly backed rebel units in the Ogaden region, an act which embarrassed the Soviet Union which had troops in Ethiopia. The Soviets promptly cut off military aid to Somalia but increased the supply of 'defence' weapons to Ethiopia. Somalia in turn expelled 1,500 Soviet military and civilian personnel and broke off diplomatic relations with Cuba which had been supplying military aid to Ethiopia.

In the subsequent eight-months war over the Ogaden, Somalia was defeated but the matter of the Ogaden is still not settled.

In 1978 the US agreed to supply $13 million of food aid to Somalia but not military aid unless Somalia gave up all claims to Northern Kenya, the Ogaden and the Republic of Djiboute (claimed also by Ethiopia). Somalia had hoped to form a Greater Somalia (all peoples of Somali origin) by uniting these territories and refused the US offer.

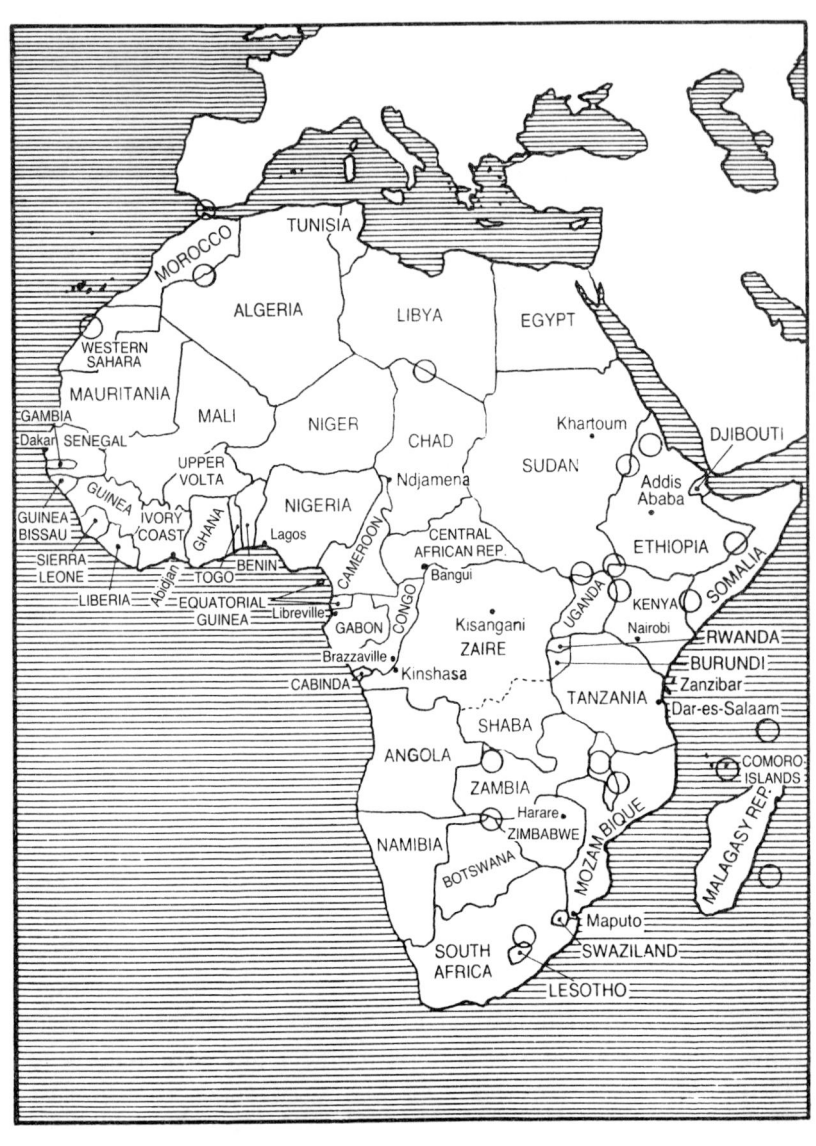

Africa's disputed frontiers (denoted by circles)

Libya

Frontier incursions between Libya and Egypt boiled over in 1977 when a four-day war broke out between the two countries, after Egypt charged Libya for attacking a frontier post. Superior Egyptian air power and armour inflicted heavy losses on Libya and the clash ended by the intervention of Algeria.[5] In its southern frontier with Chad, Libya claims that the frontier was extended by the purchase of the Aozou Strip from Chad for $120 million in 1973. Chad denied that any such sale took place and over a period of six years the matter could not be resolved whereupon Libya invaded Chad in 1979 and although repulsed invaded again a year later . In 1981 the two countries announced their intention to unite. However, France, the former colonial power, and other African countries opposed such an agreement and Libyan troops were withdrawn from Chad territory in November 1981.

In 1982 Libyan-backed rebel troops captured the Chad capital and in the following year France sent some 3,000 troops into Chad to oppose the rebels. Both French and Libyan forces were withdrawn in 1984, although some Libyan troops remained in the north until 1987 when Chad forces finally drove them out. The rebels abandoned some $1 billion of military equipment during their retreat.[6]

Morocco

The frontier between Morocco and Algeria lies along the line of, and between, the Guir and Dra Rivers. The line agreed in 1938 - The Trinquet Project Line - delineated a natural frontier but the effective line of Moroccan jurisdiction is 50-100 miles further north. French maps show the frontier even further south than the Trinquet Line. The Franco-Spanish Treaty (1912) delineated the Dra River as the frontier between Spanish Morocco and French Morocco, and in 1962 the area between the two rival frontier lines was occupied by Moroccan troops. A frontier war broke out later that year.[7]

Morocco claims large areas of Algeria, Mauretania and Mali

as a greater Moroccan state which it contends existed some generations before the colonial era when France and Spain divided the country into zones of influence. However, this claim is based on questionable historical ground. Morocco gained independence in 1956. It annexed over 70,000 square miles of phosphate-rich land in the former Spanish Sahara in 1975/76, the remainder being taken by Mauretania. Spain withdrew from the Western Sahara in 1976 and accepted this partition. The day following Spain's withdrawal, a new movement - the Polisario - came into being and its leadership proclaimed the existence of a new state, the Saharan Arab Democratic Republic (SADR) and launched attacks against both Morocco and Mauritania. They soon proved themselves an effective guerilla organisation. Morocco accepted US military and economic aid, but in 1980, when Mauretania signed a treaty with the Polisario and gave up its piece of the former Spanish Sahara, Morocco occupied the area. After many years of bitter fighting, Morocco now controls the main urban areas, but the Polisaria Front moves freely across disputed frontiers in the vast sparsely populated deserts.[8]

Other Disputes

Two disputed frontier lines between Sudan and Kenya - the Blue Line and the Red Line - forming the Ilemi Triangle on the Sudan side of the frontier remain unresolved and although Kenya maintains frontier police posts between the two lines the Red Line is now recognised as the international frontier.

A frontier dispute between Tanzania and Malawi over Lake Malawi nearly caused a conflict in the 1960s. Tanzania claimed that the frontier followed the centre line of the lake, as it had before Britain altered it to follow the bank of the lake in 1953.[9]

Ugandan claims on Sudanese and Kenyan territory were based on its pre-1902 frontiers. In the case of the Tanzanian Kagera salient, Uganda was successful in annexing the territory after invading Tanzania in 1978. It was, however, returned to Tanzania after a Tanzanian invasion of Uganda in 1979.

The Kingdom of Lesotho refuses to accept the independence of neighbouring Transkei and also has significant territorial claims on South Africa including the Orange Free State, Herschel and Matatiele in Cape Province and parts of Natal.

A territorial dispute has arisen on the Zambesi and Chobe Rivers at Kazungula. South Africa and Zimbabwe claim that the four frontiers of Namibia, Botswana, Zimbabwe and Zambia meet at a point in midstream. Botswana and Zambia, however, claim that Namibia and Zimbabwe are separated by a section of river and Botswana wishes to build a bridge over the disputed water and provide direct access to Black Africa. The present ferry crossing has been destroyed several times by South African and Zimbabwe troops because they maintain that a bridge would provide an infiltration passage for terrorists.

No serious conflict has so far been experienced between Zambia and Zaire over the disputed village of Moliro or between Malawi and Mozambique over the delineation of the frontier in the Lake Chilwa region. Both frontiers were ill-defined by the colonial powers.

A number of disputes have arisen in the Indian Ocean mainly as a result of the former colonial powers granting independence to the Ocean islands of Juan de Nova, Bassas da India, Europa, Is Glorieuses and Troemlin. Four of these are claimed by the Malagasy Republic and the other two by Mauritius. The few inhabitants of the British Indian Ocean Territory of Chagos Archipelago were evacuated in the 1970s to Mauritius to make way for the Anglo-American base on Diego Garcia. Mauritius now claims the Archipelago on the basis that it was the seat of its administration before 1965.

SOUTH AMERICA'S DISPUTED FRONTIERS

Compared with Asia, few frontiers in South America are currently under dispute, or liable to cause future conflict. Nevertheless some are still in the process of being settled, and some disputes which appear dormant now could erupt later.

Bolivia

Bolivia lost considerable slices of territory to her three neighbours, Chile, Brazil and Paraguay, amounting in all to several thousand square miles and including its only outlet to the Pacific Ocean, lost after the Pacific war of 1879-84. In 1903, a section of Bolivia's Acre province, rich in rubber, was ceded to Brazil, and in 1938 after the war with Paraguay (1932-5) Bolivia lost nearly 100,000 square miles of its Gran Chaco region.[1]

Direct access to the Pacific is one of Bolivia's greatest present day needs. In 1976, a commission was appointed to study a Chilean proposal to grant Bolivia a corridor to the sea. As Peruvian agreement would be necessary for this frontier delineation (the area under consideration was ceded by Chile to Peru after the Pacific war) Bolivia has now concentrated on claiming Arica instead of Antofagasta, which it lost to Chile.

Peru

Peru was once part of the great Incan empire and later the major vice-royalty of Spanish South America. It claimed its independence from Spain in 1821, and for a hundred years thereafter revolutions were frequent. These included a new war with Spain in 1864-66. In 1929 the dispute with Chile over Tacna and Arica was finally settled after an attempted plebiscite in 1921 failed to find a solution.²

Peru was also engaged in the Pacific War with Bolivia, with whom it formed a secret alliance against Chile. It was at the end of this war that Peru lost considerable tracts of territory and Bolivia lost Antofagasta, its only route to the sea.

Panama

Columbus visited Panama in 1502 during his fourth voyage, and the country became the principal transhipment point for Spanish treasure and supplies to and from South America.³

In 1921, when Central America revolted against Spain, Panama joined Colombia and after US proposals for canal rights over the narrow isthmus had been rejected by Colombia in 1903, Panama proclaimed its independence with US backing.⁴ For the canal rights in perpetuity, the US paid Panama $10 million and agreed to pay $250,000 annually, increased to $430,000 after devaluation of the dollar in 1933. Under a revised treaty signed in 1955, the figure increased to over $2 million annually. In exchange, the US got the Canal Zone, a 10 mile wide strip across the Isthmus, and a considerable say in Panama's affairs.

In 1977, however, the US agreed to negotiate the ultimate handing over of the canal to Panama, and two treaties were signed, one governing the transfer and the other guaranteeing the canal's neutrality. A referendum held in the same year approved the treaties by more than a two-thirds majority. The US had the right to use military force to keep the canal open and operating should it become obstructed for any reason.

On 20 December 1989 such an eventuality occurred and the United States invaded Panama with 23,000 troops to protect the canal and safeguard US citizens. Panama's self-appointed leader was removed and democracy restored following a two year's crisis during which US citizens, of which there were 35,000, were attacked and threatened and the operation of the canal was endangered. The canal was closed for the first time in its history but reopened again on 21 December when the US reiterated its commitment to hand over the canal to Panama by the year 2000.

South America's disputed frontiers (denoted by circles)

Venezuela

Venezuela claims some 50,000 square miles of neighbouring Guyana's 83,000 square miles, with the Essequibo River as its eastern frontier. The claim dates back as far as 1844 and was repeated in 1876-9 when the British dismissed it on the grounds that they had built Guyana around the river and that the line surveyed in the 1840s - the Schomburgh Line - was the frontier.[5] When submitted to arbitration in 1899, the frontier was confirmed as the Schomburgh Line. The whole issue was reopened by Venezuela in 1949 but to no avail and the whole area of Guyana to the west of the Essequibo River is still shown on Venezuelan maps as territory under claim.[6]

Ecuador

In 1941 Peru invaded Ecuador and annexed territory north of the Maranon River which had been in dispute since 1830. The US and some South American countries supported the new frontier, which effectively covered the northern, or right bank, catchment of the river, arguing that the territory was taken from Peru by force after the Spanish left the continent in the 1880s. The ensuing treaty - the Guayaquil Treaty of 1829 and the Pedemonte-Mosquera Protocol of 1830 - demarcated the frontier as the line of the Maranon River to its confluence with the Chindipe River, thence across the Huancabamba watershed to the Pacific Ocean.

Ecuador has declared the Pedemonte-Mosquera Protocol null and void, and although the United Nations has shown no interest in Ecuador's claim for the disputed territory, the expected discovery of oil in the area is certain to aggravate the dispute.

Under the 1916 Munoz Vernaza-Suarez Treaty with Colombia, Ecuador also lost a large area of land between the watershed of the Napo-Putamayo River and the Putamayo River. It still lays claim to this territory in spite of the fact that the area was ceded to Peru by Colombia in 1922 in exchange for Peru's acceptance of Colombia's Leticia corridor.[7]

Central America

Many disputed frontiers in Central America have been 'on hold' for several years. However, if, as is now possible, the South American countries claim a 200 mile coastal fishing zone, dormant or even extinct disputes are liable to arise again.

There are also current disputes still to be settled, including the US base in Cuba-Guantanama which Cuba insists must be returned in spite of being ceded to the US in 1901. The western part of the Nicaragua-Honduras frontier was delineated in 1957 but some disagreement remains. The Nicaragua-Costa Rica frontier has never been formally ratified and violence erupted there in 1978. The El Salvador-Honduras frontier, including several islands in the Gulf of Fonseca, remains to be delineated. The Guatemala-Honduras frontier, although agreed in 1933, is still under dispute; and Guatemala claims that Belize is part of Guatemala. Belize (formerly British Honduras), a British Crown Colony from 1834 until independence in 1981, and the last British colony in South America, retains British troops as security against possible Guatemalan attacks.[8]

The Falkland Islands.

The Falkland Islands and Dependencies lie some 300 miles east of the Magellan Strait at the southern end of South America. They include about 200 islands in an area of 4,700 square miles. Of the population of about 2,000, 97 per cent are of British origin. Argentina invaded the islands on 2 April 1982 under a long-standing claim for the islands. The British responded by sending a task force, and landed on the islands on 21 May. By 14 June they had regained the territory.[9]

The Falkland Islands were first occupied by the French and British in 1764-65, but the French ceded East Falkland to Spain and the Spanish evicted the British in 1770. In the 1820s Argentine took over the islands, but they too left in 1831. The British took up residence and have remained there ever since except for the brief spell of Argentinian occupation.

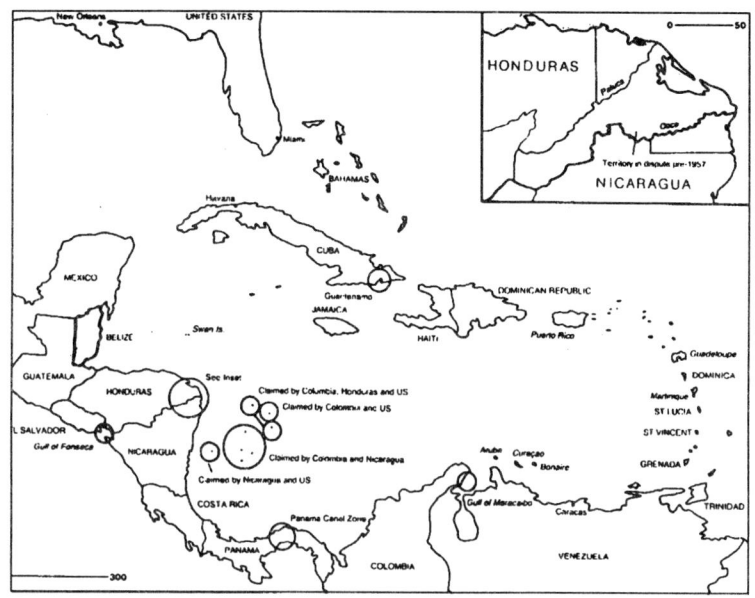

The disputed frontiers of Central America (denoted by circles)

Other Disputes

The Argentina-Chile frontier at its southward extension at Tierra del Fuego through the Beagle Channel was under dispute for a hundred years or so. It has now been resolved in favour of Chile. The dispute concerned several small islands, including Picton, Nueva, Lennox, Barnevelt and Evout. In resolving the dispute Chile, in return agreed on a 66° west frontier with Argentina to Antarctica.

Disputes in Central America continue over islands in the Caribbean involving the United States, Colombia, Honduras, Nicaragua and Venezuela. Venezuela claims the islands of Aruba, Curacao and Bonaire. On the mainland, the Nicaragua-Costa Rica frontier, the El Salvador-Honduras frontier and the Guatemala-Honduras frontier have never been formally confirmed by the countries involved.[10]

Mexican territory up until 1836 included the states of Arizona,

California, Nevada, New Mexico, Texas, Utah and parts of the states of Colorado, Kansas, Oklahoma and Wyoming. Within twelve years it had lost all of this territory except the Gadsden Purchase which the US bought in 1853 (See chapter 11).

There is no question about Mexico disputing any part of its lost territory or of any frontier adjustment, but it has incessantly complained to the US about inadequate frontier controls affecting Mexican immigrants and the US has endeavoured to stop the multi-million drug trade through the frontier.

27

ETHNIC FRONTIERS UNDER DISPUTE

It is estimated that more than 30 million people in the world today live outside their country of birth because of wars or ethnic conflict.

International frontiers are often artificial boundaries created in haste, although in good faith, but usually with a finality unacceptable to all sides when large ethnic groups are involved. The world's frontiers may confine but do not always define the many ethnic peoples, who retain their aspirations and prejudices. The frontiers of Europe today are of comparatively recent origin, founded on the Congress of Vienna (1814-15), the Peace Treaty of Paris (1919-23) and the Peace Treaties after the Second World War.

The Peace Treaties of Paris saw the break-up of the Ottoman Empire and the Austrian-Hungarian Empire. The redrawing of the frontiers of eastern Europe under these treaties failed to accommodate the aspirations of all the groups in the region. In 1923, 30 million out of 110 million people living in the region were considered minorities in their countries. By the end of the Second World War, mass killings and migration had reduced the number of ethnic minorities to 14 million, still a significant minority.[1]

The Ottoman Empire

Turkey today is a Middle East country in both Europe and Asia, and is home for 44 million of the world's 100 million ethnic Turks. Millions of Turks are scattered across a vast area in a region known as 'Turkestan' whose frontiers, if drawn on a political map, would be one of the world's largest countries, stretching from India to Siberia and from the Caspian Sea to China.[2]

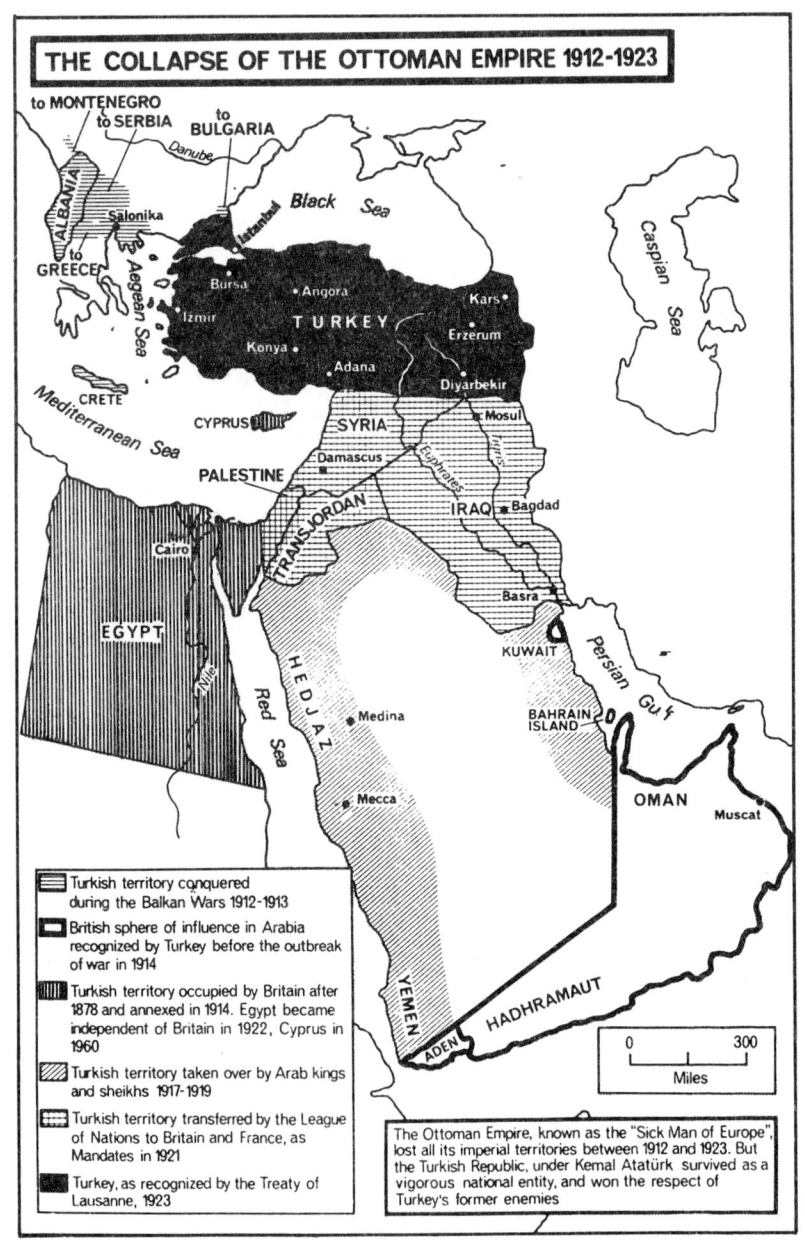

The Ottomans built an empire that ruled most of southeast Europe, North Africa and the Middle East. The Treaty of Lausanne (1919) redrew the frontiers to where they are today, but the Empire left behind many Turkish minorities in the lands it once dominated, including Iraq, Iran, Syria, Bulgaria, Greece and Cyprus. Ethnic Turks from these countries now seek recognition and independence or autonomy.

Almost all Turks are Moslems. Forty-two million of them live in the Soviet Union and seven million in China; both groups have suffered discrimination and persecution. In 1989 some 300,000 Turks fled Bulgaria to avoid ethnic strife. Turks in Azerbaijan destroyed fortifications along its 500 mile frontier with Iran; they wish to be united with Iranian Turkish minorities and the frontier to be redrawn to form an independent state. Azerbaijan Turks are also confronting Armenians in the Nogorno-Karabakh region. In Central Asia, Uzbek Turks have founded nationalistic movements to defy the central government, and in Cyprus Turks have declared a self-governing state in the north of the island (see chapter 7).

Turkey controls the head-waters of the Euphrates and Tigris Rivers and is currently exploiting the waters of these rivers which could have devastating effects on Iraq, Iran and Syria unless a water resources agreement is effected. Right-wing extremists in Turkey dream of restoring a pan-Turkish Empire which could well require the frontiers to be redrawn once again.[3]

Spain

In addition to the Gibraltar problem, Spain is still in the throes of disputes with the Basque and Catalonian separatist movements. The Basque terrorist organization (ETA) is, next to the IRA, Europe's most active and bloody extremist group, and even threatened to disrupt the last Olympic Games.

Catalonia encompasses the northeastern Spanish provinces of Gerona, Barcelona, Tarragona and Lerida. It was first granted the status of autonomy in 1932 but this was abolished by General Franco six years later. An exiled Catalonian government operated in Paris from 1945 for two years and later in Mexico. In 1979 an executive council was set up with its capital in Barcelona, although full autonomy is the ultimate aim.

The Basque country comprises an area bordering the Bay of Biscay in both Spain and France, and includes the foothills of the Pyrenees. From a total population of over one million, about 20 per cent of Basques live in France, and a further 200,000 live in emigrant communities outside Spain, in South America and the United States.

The Basques have long been a militant people and were never subdued by the Romans. The ETA separatist movement has consistently used violence in support of its struggle for self-determination, and in twenty years of fighting has killed more than 600 people.

Although so far the nationalist parties have limited themselves to demanding more political and financial power, Madrid became seriously alarmed when in September 1991 the European Commission recognised the Baltic states. This prompted Catalonia and the Basque country to claim that they have the same rights as Lithuania. One Catalonian political party even went so far as to claim independence for all Catalonian countries, including Valencia and the Balearic Islands. While the EC works towards a united Europe, the historic cultures and languages of the Basques and Catalonians may yet demand a national or regional plebiscite as a long-term solution.

Yugoslavia

Yugoslavia was carved out of the Austrian-Hungarian Empire by the Peace Conference of Paris and further frontier changes were agreed after the Second World War (see chapters 6 and 10). Except for Slovenia, none of Yugoslavia's republics was ethnically homogeneous and its restless minorities resulted on 25 June 1991 in Slovenia and Croatia declaring independence from the Yugoslav Federation.

Tito had successfully held down the six republics (Serbia,

Slovenia, Croatia, Bosnia-Hercegovina, Macedonia and Montenegro) by totalitarian power and by silencing the dissidents, of whom he sent some 7,000 to a living hell on the barren island of Goli Otok in the Adriatic. Nevertheless, Yugoslavia progressed under Tito and became arguably the most prosperous Communist country. He also gave autonomy to the provinces of Kosovo, with its Albanian majority, and Vojvodina, with a large Hungarian population.

With Communism in tatters, however, the historic hatred between Croats and Serbs came to a climax after Croatia's declaration of independence, and bloody civil war ensued, compounded by Macedonia's declaration of independence on 8 September and Bosnia-Hercegovina's declaration of independence in April 1992. Macedonian territory is claimed by Serbia, Bulgaria and Greece, and Serbia promptly served notice that it regards parts of the territory as their ancestral lands of which Skopje was in in fact the capital. Macedonia was known by Serbia as South Serbia prior to the end of the Second World War, but Greece announced in 1945 that it would not recognise any state bearing the name of that 'ancient Greek Province' and Bulgaria has never recognised Macedonia as a nation, claiming that Macedonians are all Bulgars.

Milovan Djilas, the leading Yugoslav intellectual who received an honorary doctorate from the University of Bristol for his literary contribution to history, argues that it is the border disputes in Yugoslavia which have led to what he believes will be an escalating civil war. However, it was he himself, he admits, who was asked by Tito in 1945 to delineate the border between Serbia and Croatia.[4] Djilas says that six republics were created on the basis of the Russian system, with internal borders drawn by him, and republican flags and constitutions.[5]

He acknowledges today that it was virtually impossible to delineate such borders in Yugoslavia, and as a result there was immediate conflict between Serb and Croat Communists. The Croats, he says, whose medieval state collapsed in the year 1102, claimed that their border reached as far as Zemun, a suburb of Belgrade. The medieval kingdom of the Serbs collapsed three centuries later, and they had different ideas. In the end the ethnic majority decided the issue, and the River Danube became the border to Vukovar, then south to Sid and the River Sava. This border left Serbian villages on the Western side of the Danube and around Vukovar. Djilas says that it was decided to give these villages to Croatia. On the other hand, there were some 180,000 Croats living around Subotica inside Serbia and to-day 140,000 Serbs live in Zagreb, the Croatian capital, but the border was accepted by

Yugoslavia, 1991

both republics.[6]

Yugoslavia, it must be argued, was artificially created, mainly by Britain, at the end of the First World War as a reward to the Serbs for being an ally. It was on 28 June 1914 that Austria declared war on Serbia after Geyrilo Princip, a young Bosnian Serb, assassinated Archduke Franz Ferdinand, heir to the Austria-Hungarian throne. The country became known originally in 1918 as the Kingdom of Serbs Croats and Slovenes on the break-up of the Austro-Hungarian Empire. It was handicapped right from the start by three religions (Catholic, Orthodox and Islam), half a dozen languages and six main races. In addition, the ethnic pattern did not follow the provincial borders, with minorities in enclaves within the major components. During the Second World War the hostility between the races broke out into a civil war in which some 10 per cent of the population were killed, mainly by the Ustashi, the Nazi-backed Croat government forces and by the Chetniks, the nationalist Serbs. Today an invisible line still runs through the country: north and west tends to central European culture, and south and east to the Balkans, for centuries under the Ottoman Empire. The same line virtually

The Partition of Yugoslavia, 1941

delineates the frontier of the old Austro-Hungarian Empire.[7]

However, as well as disagreement between Serbia, Croatia and Slovenia, the conflict is also concerned with the dilemma posed by Serbs who live in Croatia and Albanians who live in Serbia. The restless province of Kosovo, Serbia's southern province, an ethnic Albanian majority of nearly two million has opposed all Belgrade's moves to initiate direct rule and in a period of eighteen months in 1989/90 some sixty Albanians were killed in clashes with Serbian security units. Serbia has wiped out Kosovo's autonomy by force and cannot accept losing the province to a non-Slavic, non-orthodox people whom they refer to as 'overbearing defilers'. Long before becoming a federation, Yugoslavia was seriously troubled by tribal vendettas between its myriad ethnic groups. However, it was held together by the monarchy between the wars and by Tito's brand of Communism from the Second World War until his death in 1980. Kosova Albanians clamour for their own republic, with new frontiers, equal in status to Serbia. Ethnic Albanians are mainly Moslems, Europe's fastest growing ethnic population, and form some 90 per cent of Kosovo's people.

Populations and ethnic minorities in the six Yugoslav States[8]

Bosnia-Hercegovina:	Population 4.2 million: majority Muslims, 48% Slavs, 31%
Croatia:	Population 4.5 million: majority Croats with 600,000 Serbs, 19% Croats
Macedonia:	Population 2 million: 68% Macedonian, 25% Albanian
Montenegro:	Population 0.5 million
Serbia:	Population 9.3 million, 40% non Serb, ethnic Hungarians in north and Albanians in south: Two provinces Vojvodina and Kosovo
Slovenia:	Population 2 million, 90% Slovene

The Soviet Union

Three dramatic events over a period of fifteen days in 1991 rocked the world and saw the disintegration of the Soviet Empire.

First, Mikhail Gorbachev's six years of perestroika almost ended in disaster when a Communist coup d'etat erupted in Moscow on 19 August. Fortunately this lasted only three days, thanks mainly to the dogged resistance of Boris Yeltsin, President of the Russian Republic. Second, on the 24 August the Soviet Communist Party was suspended by the Congress of the People's Deputies. Third, only nine days later, the Soviet Union's supreme legislative body voted overwhelmingly to bury the existing union of fifteen Soviet republics. The USSR would become a Confederation of Sovereign States. The Congress of People's Deputies, the supreme legislature of the Soviet Union, was bundled into oblivion three days later.

The new federation would be based on the principles of independence and 'territorial integrity' – a necessary inclusion

The 15 republics of the former Soviet Union
(now the Commonwealth of Independent States)

since some twenty internal borders are being contested, and these may well become frontiers and flash-points of future conflict. It is believed that Boris Yeltsin raised the matter of the borders of the Russian Republic because at least 30 million Russians live in non-Russian republics, a situation similar to that existing in Yugoslavia between Croats and Serbs but on a much greater scale.

The downfall of Communism in the former Soviet Union may

yet have a knock-on effect on other Communist regimes, especially China with its dormant border disputes in Tibet and Inner Mongolia. Although China has enjoyed political stability and unity among its fifty-five minorities which make up some 7 per cent of the population (35 million people), the disintegration of the Soviet Union must heighten its fears that ethnic nationalism could fuel separatism in some regions.

Communism had kept nationalistic and ethnic passions in check, but now old resentments and quarrels are resurgent in practically every newly independent state. The Soviet Moslem population, neglected by Moscow for years, is one of the world's largest Islamic blocks. They are the second largest group after ethnic Russians, whom they are expected to outnumber within thirty years, and are concentrated in Azerbaijan in the Caucasus and in the five Central Asian states – Uzbekistan, which has the highest birth-rate in the world, Kazakhstan, Tadzhikistan, Turkmenistan and Kirghizia, whose southern capital, Osh, is known as the 'second Mecca'.[9]

The rising tide of Islamic fundamentalism is of concern to the new independent states and a serious situation could develop. Violence has already flared up within the last few years, and in 1989 Uzbeks attacked Meskhetian Turks whose ancestors were from Georgia. Fighting took place in Kazakhstan and Tadzhikistan, and in Kirghizia there was a serious dispute over water rights. In 1990, fighting erupted between Azerbaijan and Armenia over the disputed frontiers of Nagorno-Karabakh – an area actually in Azerbaijan although 80 per cent of the 200,000 population are ethnic Armenian. Also in 1990, Soviet tanks rolled into Dushanbe, the capital of Tadzhikistan, to put down clashes after people went on the rampage because of rumours that the city's best houses were going to Armenian refugees from Azerbaijan rather than to Tadzhiks who had been on the waiting-list for years. At a meeting in Kazakhstan in 1990, political leaders, seeing the danger of civil war in the region, appealed for an end to the ethnic conflict, and in Kirghizia a democratic movement was subsequently set up with the aim of fighting for independence and calling for struggle against Communist party rule, the restoration of language, history and culture, and sovereignty within a Soviet confederation.

The independence of the Baltic states of Estonia, Latvia and Lithuania was recognised by the European Commission on 10 September 1991 after fifty years of occupation. When Germany collapsed in 1918, the three Baltic states were recognised by Britain and the United States, and subsequently by Russia, who proclaimed the right of self-determination. However, this did not last long. Britain and France had to intervene, and blockaded Petrograd (Leningrad, now St. Petersburg) and sent marines into Estonia.

With this protection, the three Baltic states maintained their independence until 1939 when they came under the Hitler-Stalin pact. As soon as the Second World War broke out Soviet troops marched into all three countries and they were formally annexed in 1940. A year later they were re-occupied by the Nazis and in 1944-5 by Stalin. During the war, the Jews were massacred and the educated one-third of the population was deported to the Soviet interior. However, many escaped to the West.

After 1945 masses of people were deported, native languages were swamped when Russians or Ukrainians moved in, and churches became museums. Communism, backed by force, suppressed any hint of disobedience. Nevertheless, it is now known that the people of the three states never gave up seeking their freedom and went on fighting in their own quiet way by placing men in high administrative posts in Vilna, Riga and Tallinn. On 17 September, one week after their independence, all three countries were admitted to the United Nations in a moving flag raising ceremony in New York.

After a referendum in December, the Ukraine, shaking off three centuries of Russian rule, also declared its independence. In so doing, it became the fifth largest country in Europe, with a population of some 52 million and an area of 233,000 square miles.

Within a week the frontiers of Europe were further redrawn

when three states, Byelorussia, Russia and the Ukraine, founded the Commonwealth of Independent States. The Union of Soviet Socialist Republics had ceased to exist. On Christmas Day, 1991, Mikhail Gorbachev's seven year reign finally ended. In this short period he had changed the map of the world.

Populations and ethnic minorities in the fifteen former Soviet republics[10]

Russia	145,000,000,	83% Russian, 17% divided among 38 minorities
Ukraine	51,704,000,	74% Ukrainian, 21% Russian, 1% Jewish
Byelorussia	10,200,000,	79% Byelorussian, 12% Russian, 4% Polish
Moldavia	4,341,000,	64% Moldavian, 14% Ukrainian, 13% Russian
Armenia	3,283,000,	90% Armenian, 5.3% Azerbaijani, 2.3% Russian
Azerbaijan	7,000,000,	78% Azerbaijani, 7.9% Russian, 7.9% Armenian
Georgia	5,449,000,	69% Georgian, 9% Armenian, 7% Russian
Kazakhstan	16,536,000,	41% Russian, 36% Kazakh, 6% Ukrainian
Uzbekistan	19,906,000,	69% Uzbek, 11% Russian, 4% Tatar
Turkmenistan	3,534,000,	68% Turkmenian, 13% Russian, 9% Uzbek
Tadzhikistan	5,112,000,	59% Tajik, 23% Uzbek, 6% Russian
Kirghizia	4,291,000,	48% Kirghizian, 26% Russian, 12% Uzbek
Lithuania	3,690,000,	80% Lithuanian, 9% Russian, 8% Polish
Latvia	2,681,000,	54% Latvian, 33% Russian, 13% Others
Estonia	1,573,000,	65% Estonian, 28% Russian, 3% Ukrainian

Georgia did not immediately join the Commonwealth, however, and was immersed in a bloody civil war. Georgia has been on a collision course with the Kremlin since October 1990 when the nationalist coalition won a parliamentary election. The first acts of the new parliament were to drop the words 'Soviet' and 'Socialist' from the Republics's name. Georgia's Communist party broke with the central Soviet party and, committed to working for the restoration of the Republic's sovereignty, sent only 10 per cent of its quota of conscripts to the armed forces. In the ethnic enclave of the South Ossetian Autonomous Region in Georgia, Moscow was charged with fanning unrest and supporting a 'Soviet Democratic Republic of South Ossetian'. The parliament in Tbilisi, capital of Georgia, responded by dissolving the autonomous region altogether and sent in police reinforcements. Skirmishes resulted in twelve deaths. In January 1991 Gorbachev refused to support parliament's decision and gave Georgia a three-day ultimatum to withdraw their police units from South Ossetia. Georgia ignored the ultimatum.

In January 1991 a conference on human rights held in Vienna under the auspices of the Council of Europe heard that the exodus from the Soviet Union and its satellites could involve up to 30 million people and become the biggest population upheaval Europe has seen since the Second World War. Hungary has already taken 40,000 refugees from the East. Austria has processed 600,000 refugees since 1945, and there are still over 1,000 refugees living in its Traiskirchen refugee camp.

The Iron Curtain obviated the need for East-West immigration controls, but now ethnic migration is gaining pace in the new atmosphere of change and instability, especially where these minority groups are under pressure. There are 3 million people of German stock still living in the Eastern bloc, 1.5 million Jews, 3.5 million Armenians, 650,000 Turks and nearly 4 million gypsies. Millions of Poles and peoples of other nationalities became Soviet citizens when frontiers were redrawn after the Second World War. Moldavia's Russian-speaking population, concentrated on the eastern bank of the River Dniester, and the Gagauz Turk minority in the south, have both declared independence from the republic which has an ethnic Romanian majority and which may push for merging with Romania. Three people were killed when Moldavian Interior Ministry troops cleared the Dniester Bridge of barricades at Dubossry in November 1990.

The Winter War in Finland in 1939, and its successor two years later, have left a deep scar on the people of Finnish Karelia. Twenty-two thousand Finnish soldiers died in the winter campaign during which temperatures dropped to -45° C. The eastern half of Karelia was duly ceded to the Soviet

Union in 1940, and today, over fifty years later, the people of Karelia want the region returned to Finland and the frontier redrawn. Finnish officials have warned that as many as 2 million people may try to cross the frontier in an exodus from the unrest and bleak future in the former Soviet Union.[11]

Ethnic unrest is everywhere: in Europe, on the Indian continent, in the Middle East, Southeast Asia, the South Pacific, South America and in Canada where French-speaking separatists want Quebec to become an independent state. The 280 million people of what was once the former Soviet Union, however, are heading towards an especially uncertain future as the world's last great empire lies in tatters. It could take years before the newly-formed Commonwealth of Independent States negotiate their way through a minefield of territorial disputes and ethnic quarrels.

Belgium

Ethnic nationalism is threatening to split the Belgian state in two - Flanders and Wallonia with French-speaking Brussels isolated in the middle. All the major political parties in Flanders are now ready to break away from the Francophone Walloons of the south, and the 6 million Flemish speakers have no doubt that they are now economically subsidising the 4 million French speakers. So autonomous do they wish to become that the Flemings want to negotiate their own international treaties and even wish to see Flanders represented in the World Cup and Olympics.[12]

The border between the two communities (or 'the Language Frontier', though the problem concerns much more than a language difference) was officially drawn in 1962. To the north of this line the language is Flemish, to all intents and purposes Dutch. To the south of the border, French is the language, though, as in the north, with a variety of accents. The forces which once held the two communities together were Roman Catholicism and economic and political opposition to the Dutch, but these are apparently no longer strong enough to maintain unity. The Kingdom of Belgium dates only from 1831. Because

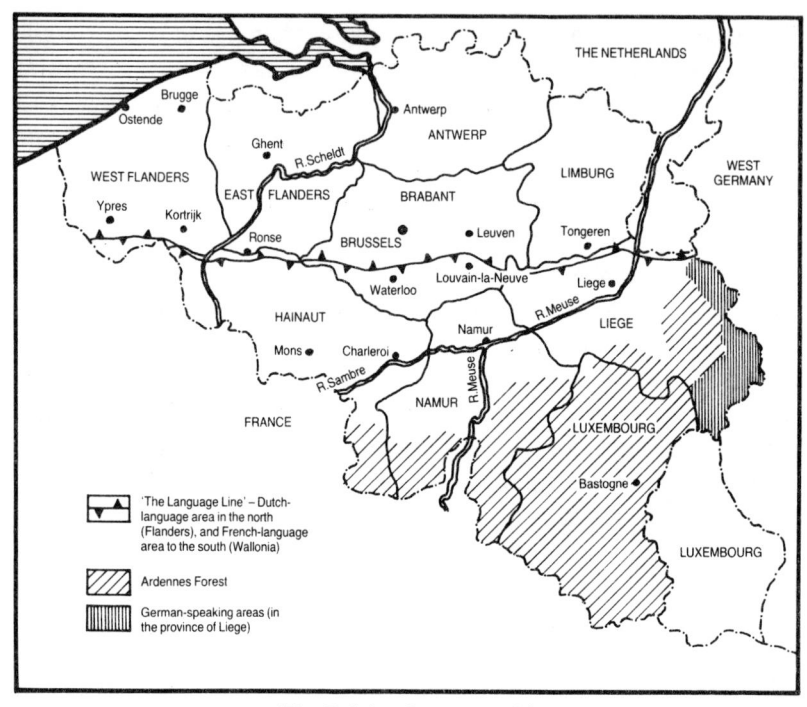

The Belgian Language Line

of the way the country has evolved, both historically and geographically, it has no natural frontiers, such as mountain chains or large rivers, and has therefore always been vulnerable to invasion.

During the last 200 years there have been three distinct periods in Belgian history:

The Austrian Habsburgs (1713-94), when Belgium was known as the Austrian Netherlands, and, although under Austrian rule, remained substantially independent as it had done under Spain (1579-1713). It was during this period that Maria Theresa reigned over the Austrian Empire, and, under her popular governor, Charles of Lorraine, roads and waterways were built and agriculture modernised.[13]

Under French Annexation (1794-1814), measures were ruthlessly enforced but the annexation did at least have the effect of transforming Belgium into a modern state. The church was persecuted and other highly unpopular dictates led to the Peasant's Revolt in October 1798. Under Napoleon, the metric system was introduced and the Scheldt reopened. The revival of the port of Antwerp and industrial development enabled the country to profit from markets available in the French Empire. In spite of all their improvements the French were unpopular and the Allied occupation of the country was welcomed after the fall of Napoleon in 1814.[14]

The United Kingdom of the Netherlands (1815-1831): the Allies amalgamated Belgium and Holland into the United Kingdom of the Netherlands under Prince William of Orange, mainly to deter any further French expansion. Although William was extremely pro-Dutch, industry flourished, Antwerp prospered, and education advanced. But there was much that Belgians did not accept: the country's population was double that of Holland's, but they were forced to have equal representation at state level, to speak Dutch as the official language and to respect the authority of a foreign Protestant king.

Revolution duly broke out in 1830, and at the London Conference on 20 January 1831 Belgium was recognised as an independent and 'perpetually neutral' state. A frontier was duly demarcated between the Netherlands and Belgium. However, William would not accept the London Agreement and invaded within a few days of the conference. He captured Antwerp, evacuating it only after French troops were called in to blockade Dutch ports and carry out an assault on the city.

Not until 1839 did William accept defeat, and the independence and neutrality of Belgium was finally sealed by the Treaty of London (1839). This treaty was signed by Austria, Britain, Prussia, France and Russia, later to become known as the 'scrap of paper.' The Dutch, who disputed the frontier drawn in London in 1831, were now awarded a slice of northern Belgium and Belgium was compensated by a grant of half of Luxembourg's territory. The settlement satisfied everyone except Luxembourg, which had lost 25 per cent of its country between 1815 (the Congress of Vienna) and 1839 (the Treaty of London).

After the First World War the Belgian frontier was again modified by the addition of the German-speaking areas of Eupen, Malmedy and Saint Vith (by plebiscite, see chapter 28), and a League of Nations mandate over two former German colonies in Africa, now called Rwanda and Burundi. There seems no solution to this purely ethnic problem in this rich and historic country and the ethnic Frontier through Ypres, Ronse, Waterloo, Waremme and Tongeren, now only a concept, could eventually become a reality.

Postscript
As this book goes to press, few disputed borders have been resolved. If anything further disputes have arisen. China has claimed a huge swath of the South China Sea extending to more than 1,000 miles south of the nearest populated Chinese island. The area includes island groups reputedly rich in minerals but is also claimed by Vietnam and other countries. In 1974 Chinese and Vietnamese forces fought a naval battle over the territory.

In the former Soviet Union there are now some 50 different minority groups in the new states and 160 border disputes. Of the 23 frontiers dividing the new republics, only three are not contested. In Yugoslavia others may be drawn into a civil war which has no logic and no winners and new border disputes will inevitably arise.

The long standing frontier dispute between El Salvador and Honduras has, however, been settled by the International Court of Justice in the Hague and disputed territory totalling 168 square miles has been shared between the two states, Honduras receiving two-thirds of the area with the Bay of Fonseca to be shared with Nicaragua.

Water remains one of the key issues of dispute between Arab and Israeli and since the latter abstracts more than half its fresh water from the West Bank it is unlikely it will give up its control of that region. Iraq and Syria are in dispute with Turkey and Egypt has accused Sudan and Ethiopa of abstracting Nile water needed for Egyptian irrigation.

28

PLEBISCITES AS A SOLUTION ?

Plebiscites have been used to good effect as a fair means of determining frontiers where disputes have arisen over territorial rights. During the Paris Peace Conference (1919-23) the Great Powers found that the plebiscite met the Wilson requirements of self-determination of the peoples involved in the various frontier disputes.

The principle that a plebiscite gives freedom of choice to both sides in the dispute was clearly established by the plebiscites carried out during and after this period. It may be argued, however, that a plebiscite merely confirms a cession or annexation already made by treaty, but this has not been the case in those carried out in Europe since the First World War.[1] In seven official plebiscites undertaken according to strict rules, the majority vote went in favour of the vanquished country and against the proposed cession. In all seven cases the vanquished country was either Germany or Austria-Hungary. In addition seven unilateral referenda or consultations were undertaken, although in some cases those were unofficial and purely internal. Both the plebiscites and consultations are summarised in the following tables.[2]

Adjustments to existing frontiers in accordance with the results of the plebiscites, or unilateral consultations, were necessary in most, but not all, of the cases.

Plebiscites were refused by the Great Powers, however, for South Tirol and Hungary, and no explicit reasons were given.

Although there are great practical difficulties in the application of a plebiscite there are also distinct advantages. In principle

PLEBISCITES

Date	Area	Population (1920)	Sovereignty before plebiscite	Plebiscite won by	Other country involved in claim
1920	Schleswig	274,000	Germany	Denmark Zone 1 Germany Zone 2	Denmark
1920	Allenstein	560,000	Germany	Germany	Poland
1920	Marienwerde	161,000	Germany	Germany	Poland
1920	Southern Carinthia	126,000	Austria	Austria	Yugoslavia
1921	Sopron	48,000	Hungary	Hungary	Austria
1921	Upper Silesia	2,000,000	Germany	Germany	Poland
1935	Saar	800,000	Germany	Germany	France

UNILATERAL CONSULTATIONS

Date	Area	Population	Sovereignty before Vote	Sovereignty after Vote
1919	Vorarlberg	40,000	Austria	Austria (1)
1919-21	Mosul	800,000	Turkey	Iraq
1920	Eupen	37,000	Germany	Belgium
1920	Malmedy	27,000	Germany	Belgium
1921	Tirol	150,000	Austria	Austria (2)
1921	Salzburg	105,000	Austria	Austria (2)
1922	Vilnius	390,000	Poland	Poland (3)

Notes:

(1) Internal referendum for voluntary annexation to Switzerland.
(2) Internal referendum for voluntary annexation to Germany.
(3) Consultation won over Lithuania.

the solution by plebiscite is the fairest one for all concerned, but much depends on the methods employed. The question actually put to the voters is obviously of the utmost importance; the time permitted for propaganda is often difficult to judge; and the method of assessing the results of the voting can be critical. In the case of Upper Silesia the result might have been very different if the voters had had the option of voting for an autonomous state. In southern Carinthia the voting was taken in a single zone and the total majority assessed over the whole zone. If the voting had been by communes, however, the Austrian territory south of the River Drau would today be in Yugoslavia. Historical aspects of the territory in dispute also require careful consideration. In the case of Eupen and Malmedy, Germany insisted that these districts never belonged to Belgium or to any of the political formations which could be considered as predecessors of Belgium.

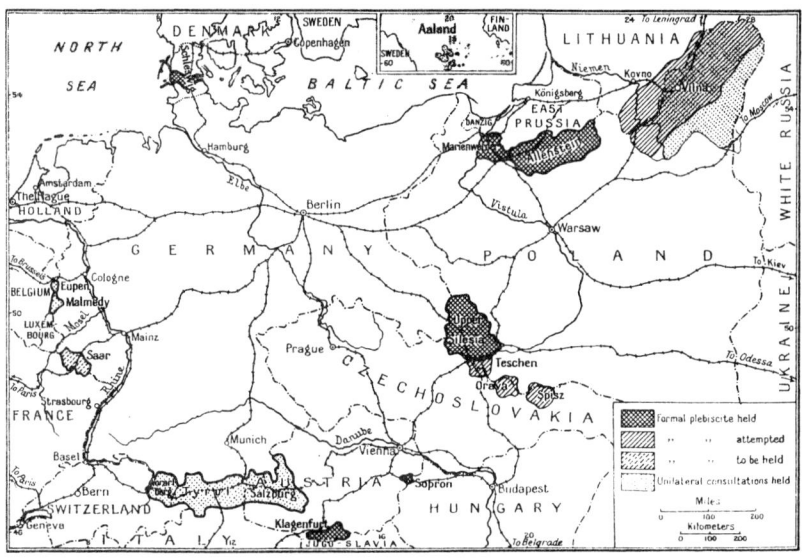

Plebiscites and Consultations held, attempted, or planned in Europe 1914-1939

Unfortunately, no matter what the result, there has always been a protest by the losing party; normally this has taken the form of criticism of the manner in which the plebiscite has been conducted. Sometimes accusations were made that the registers had been falsified, or that there had been duplication of voting certificates, or that voters were intimidated to the extent that they refused to go to the polls.

The difficulties involved in assessing a plebiscite are illustrated in the case of the village of Tarrenz in Austria. In 1938, the Austrian government's proposed plebiscite for Austrian independence from Germany was cancelled by order of Hitler. Because of poor communications, the village did not learn of the cancellation and proceeded with the voting.

One hundred per cent of the electorate voted for Austrian independence. A few weeks later, under a Hitler plebiscite, one hundred per cent of the electorate voted for the Anschluss (union with Germany).[3]

It is often difficult to assess how a person will vote, and this sometimes leads to disappointment of the losing party and often to accusations that voters have been pressurised.

The assumption that a person will vote according to his or her mother tongue has been shown to be invalid. The results of voting in the southern Carinthian plebiscite, in which the majority of Slovenes voted for Austria, were the exact opposite of what the language figures suggested. It is true, however, that a strong tendency exists for racial groups to band together but even so there are other important factors. Not everyone is a strong nationalist; the wish of the people to retain their jobs and provide for their families is often more important.[4]

In Europe nationalism probably receives more support from intellectuals, writers, teachers and clergy than it does from the commercial and industrial community who are more concerned with their markets. The economic argument has probably more bearing on these voters than language or nationality. An example of economic factors being predominant over nationalism is found in the referenda carried out in Austria after the First World War. In 1919 the Austrian National Assembly protested against the ban placed on them by the Great Powers on union with Germany, and wished to exercise their right of self-determination.

The call for union, or Anschluss, was taken up on both sides of the frontier, and Karl Renner led the struggle from the Austrian side that German Austria should join the German Reich. Accordingly, the Austrian Government in 1921 organized referenda on a regional basis (see table above). The results in

Tirol and Salzburg were as follows:[5]

Tirol: For union with Germany............ 145,302
Against 1,805

Salzburg: For union with Germany.............. 98,546
Against 877

Faced with threats that Carinthia would be occupied by Yugoslavia, the Federal Government banned further provincial referenda.

Two years earlier, Vorarlberg had claimed self-determination and proclaimed the right to cede to Switzerland. The Swiss Federal Council advised the province to carry out a plebiscite. This was held on 11 May 1919 and gave a majority for union with Switzerland of 47,208 votes to 11,248 - a 80 per cent majority.

The Great Powers opposed any form of further dismemberment of the country and provided adequate financial loans to the Austrian Government to see the country through its most difficult period of economic recession.

As a postscript to this post-war period of unrest in Austria, in 1930 Dr Otto Ender, the Landeshauptmann of Vorarlberg, who had issued the call for the union with Switzerland and organized the referendum, was made Chancellor of Austria.

There were to be no further modifications to the frontiers of Austria and they remain today as they were delineated by the Treaty of St Germain.

There is little doubt the plebiscite can be a device of great usefulness but, no matter how appealing, it can never become a universal rule of thumb. There will always remain certain areas where disputes over sovereignty or frontiers cannot be settled by this means, especially if enclaves are too small to be independent states or too remote to be attached to a state of the same nationality.

EPILOGUE

As this book goes to press, Europe watches anxiously the collapse of Yugoslavia, the dissolution of the Soviet Union and many other minor ethnic struggles. The settlement of these momentous problems are outside the scope of plebiscites or referenda. There are too many people scattered in too many enclaves to make for tidy frontiers and political and ethnic autonomy.

The European Community, although showing good intentions in these crises, has yet to achieve something concrete. The thirty-five nation Conference on Security and Cooperation in Europe (CSCE) has been neutered from the start by the necessity of unanimity (Yugoslavia as a member has a veto). An idea which has gained recent support is to revise the 19th century idea of 'the Concert of Europe' which revolved around the six great powers of the day (Britain, France, Russia, Austria-Hungary and later Germany and Italy in the present century).[1] The Concert accepted that they had obligations to each other and to Europe, and although they imposed a fairly authoritarian and reactionary peace, from the time of the Battle of Waterloo until the murder of Archduke Ferdinand in Sarajevo, there was peace in Europe. The success of the Concert was due to the fact that the great powers were able to produce and impose a solution when events threatened peace and stability.

It would seem, however, that the politicians have already the institutions available to them for containing, or even solving (if that is possible), the explosive potential of ethnic and territorial disputes in central and Eastern Europe and the former Soviet Union. These include the UN Security Council, the European Community, the CSCE, the Council of Europe, the Court of Human Rights, the Western European Union and NATO. A European Bill of Rights for minorities, founded by these insitutions and with sufficient military teeth, is desirable. Although force may become necessary in some circumstances to enforce the rules, by that time it may be too late anyway. There was sufficient warning available to the politicians of the impending danger of conflict in Yugoslavia, but there was no established institution that could immediately address the problem of territorial or minority rights and contain what became a bloody revolution.[2]

At a unique summit meeting of the UN Security Council on 31 January 1992, however, in the presence of the five permanent members, the Secretary General was authorized to embark on a role of peacemaker and peace-keeper with powers to intervene in all disputes in any corner of the globe. Time will tell if the rhetoric can be transformed into performance.

NOTES

Chapter 1

1. Nyrop, R.F.
2. *The Treaties of Peace*, 1919-1923, Carnegie Endowment for International Peace, New York, 1924
3. *New Civil Engineer*, 14 Nov, 1991
4. Nyrop, R.F.
5. *The Daily Telegraph*, March 4, 1988
6. *The European*, Feb 6 - 12, 1992
7. Nyrop, R.F.
8. Ibid
9. Ibid
10. *Newsweek*, March 11, 1991

Chapter 2

1. *The World Almanac*
2. Ibid

Chapter 3

1. *Berlin in Brief*
2. Ibid
3. Ibid
4. Ibid
5. Ibid
6. *The Daily Telegraph*, Oct 3, 1990
7. *Berlin in Brief*
8. Ibid
9. Ibid

10 Ibid
11 *The Daily Telegraph,* Oct 3, 1990

Chapter 4

1 *The Treaties of Peace*, 1919-1923, Carnegie of Endowment for International Peace, New York, 1924
2 *The New York Times International*, Nov 12, 1990
3 *The Treaties of Peace*, 1919-1923, Carnegie Endowment for International Peace, New York, 1924
4 Wambaugh, Sarah
5 *The Times*, Aug 18, 1990
6 *Newsweek*, Nov 26, 1990

Chapter 5

1 *The Treaties of Peace*, 1919-1923, Carnegie Endowment for International Peace, New York, 1924
2 *The New York Times International*, Oct 25, 1990
3 *Prognosis*, Czechoslovakia, Sept 1991
4 Ibid

Chapter 6

1 *The Treaties of Peace*, 1919 - 1923, Carnegie Endowment for International Peace, New York, 1924
2 Wambaugh, Sarah
3 *The European*, July 19-21, 1991
4 Temperley, H.W.V.
5 *The European*, July 19-21, 1991

Chapter 7

1 *The World Almanac*
2 *The Daily Telegraph*, Aug 15, 1991

Chapter 8

1 *The Daily Telegraph*, Oct 19, 1990

Chapter 9

1 *Der Spiegel*, Nov 1990
2 Nelson, H.D.
3 *Newsweek*, March 26, 1990 June 24, 1991
4 *The Daily Express*, March 17, 1990
5 Ibid
6 *The New York Times International*, Nov 9, 1990

Chapter 10

1 *The Treaties of Peace*, 1919-1923, Carnegie Endowment for International Peace, New York, 1924
2 Ibid
3 Macmillan, Harold, *Tides of Fortune*, Macmillan, London, 1969
4 *Kleine Zeitung*, Graz, Austria, 5 June, 1990
5 Herschy, Reg
6 Ibid

Chapter 11

1 Morris, R.B.
2 Ibid
3 *National Geographic*, Feb 1990

Chapter 12

1 *The World Almanac*

Chapter 13

1. Bunge, F.M.
2. Ibid
3. *The Daily Telegraph*, Sept 7, 1990

Chapter 14

1. Royle, Trevor
2. *Newsweek*, Jan 14, 1991
3. *The Daily Telegraph*, Feb 8, 1992

Chapter 15

1. Woodman, Dorothy
2. Ibid
3. Barthorp, M., *The North-West Frontier*, Blanford Press, 1982

Chapter 16

1. *The New Encyclopaedia Britannica*, 1988
2. Fitzgerald, W.
3. *The Daily Telegraph*, May 28, 1991

Chapter 17

1. Bunge, F.M.
2. *The Daily Telegraph*, April 3, 1991

Chapter 18

1. The Dalai Lama, *Freedom in Exile*, Curtis, Hodder and Stoughton, 1990
2. Woodman, Dorothy

Chapter 19

1 *International Herald Tribune*, March 27, 1991
2 *The Independent*, 19 April, 1991
3 *The New York Times International*, Oct 31, 1990

Chapter 20

1 *The World Almanac*

Chapter 21

1 *National Geographic*, April 1987
2 *The Daily Telegraph*, Nov 26, 1990
3 Ibid

Chapter 22

1 Hills, George
2 Ibid
3 Ibid

Chapter 23

1 Foreign and Commonwealth Office, *Private Communication*, 17 June 1991
2 Ibid
3 Ibid

Chapter 24

1 Hickey and Doherty
2 *The Times*, March 25, 1991

Chapter 25

1 Downing, David
2 *Sudan*, A Country Study
3 *Ethiopa*, A Country Study
4 Downing, David
5 *The Daly Telegraph*, Nov 30, Dec 3, 1990, *The New York Times*, Nov 12, 1990
6 *Libya*, A Country Study
7 *Morocco*, A Country Study
8 Keegan and Wheatcroft
9 Downing, David

Chapter 26

1 Downing, David
2 *Peru*, A Country Study
3 *The World Alamanac*
4 Ibid
5 *Venezuela*, A Country Study
6 Downing, David
7 Ibid
8 Ibid
9 *The World Almanac*
10 Keegan and Wheatcroft

Chapter 27

1 *Newsweek*, Nov 26, 1990, Jan 7, 1991
2 *The Plain Truth*
3 Ibid
4 *The European*, Sept 6-8, 1991
5 Ibid
6 Ibid
7 Temperley, H.W.V.
8 *The Daily Telegraph*, May 8, 1991
9 *The Daily Telegraph*, Feb 4, 1991
10 *The European*, Aug 30 - Sept 1, 1991

11 *The European*, June 29 - 1 July, 1990
12 *The Daily Telegraph*, Feb 4, 1991
13 Cappelaere, A., *Private Communication*, Vormingscursus voor Toeristische, Gidsen Staad Poperinge, Belgium
14 Ibid

Chapter 28

1 Wambaugh, Sarah
2 Ibid
3 Schussnig, Kurt von, *The Brutal Takeover*, Weidenfeld and Nicolson, 1969
4 Wambaugh, Sarah
5 Ibid

Epilogue

1 *The European*, Sept 6 - 8, 1991
2 *International Herald Tribune*, Sept 10, 1991

BIBLIOGRAPHY

CHAPTER 1 Disputed Frontiers of the Gulf

Nyrop, Richard F. (ed), *Persian Gulf States: A Country Study*, Washington DC, GPO for the American University, 1984.
The Daily Telegraph, January 1991
The New York Times, October, November 1990
Newsweek, January 1991
Time Magazine, December 1990
Treaty of Sèvres, 1920
Treaty of Lausanne, 1923

CHAPTER 2 Palestine's Disputed Frontiers

The World Almanac, Newspaper Enterprise Association Inc. New York, 1988
The New York Times, October, November 1990
The Daily Telegraph, October 1990
Heller, Mark A., *A Palestinian State. The Implications for Israel*, Harvard University Press, Cambridge, Mass, 1983
Time Magazine, December 1990

CHAPTER 3 The Berlin Wall

National Geographic, April 1990
Berlin in brief, Informationzentrum, Berlin, 1985
The New York Times, November 1990
The Daily Telegraph, September 1990

CHAPTER 4 Transylvania's Disputed Frontiers

The Treaty of Trianon, 1920
The Treaty of St Germain-en-Laye, 1919
The Times, August 1990
The Daily Telegraph, October 1990
Magyar Hirlap, June 1990
Pesti Hirlap, June 1990

CHAPTER 5 Czechoslovakia's Historic frontiers

The Treaty of Versailles, 1919
The Treaty of St Germain-en-Laye, 1919
Temperley, H.W.V., *A History of the Peace Conference of Paris*, Vols. V and VI, Henry Frowle and Hodder and Stoughton, 1924
The New York Times, October 1990
Fitzgerald, W., *The New Europe*, Methuen, 1946

CHAPTER 6 The Disputed Frontiers of Austria

The Treaty of St Germain-en-Laye, 1919
The Treaty of London, 1915
The Treaty of Versailles, 1919
The Treaty of Rapallo, 1920
The Austrian State Treaty, 1955
Temperley, H.W.V., *The History of the Peace Conference of Paris*, Vol V, Oxford Univ Press, 1924
Herschy, Reg, *Freedom at Midnight, Austria 1938-55 A story of the Traumatic Years of Occupation*, SPA, 1989
Nyrop, Richard F. (ed), *Yugoslavia: A Country Study*, Washington DC, GPO for the American University, 1982.
Fitzgerald, W., *The New Europe*, Methuen, 1946

CHAPTER 7 The Attila Line

Panteli, Stavros, *A New History of Cyprus*, East West Publications, 1984
Polyviou, Polyvios, *Cyprus, Conflict and Negotiation 1960-80* Gerald Duckworth, 1980.
The World Almanac, Newspaper Enterprise Association Inc., New York, 1975
Robertson, Ian, *Cyprus*, Blue Guide Ed A & C Black, 1987
Keesing's Contemporary Archives, 1976
Vocke, Harold, *The Lebanese War*, C Hunt and Company, 1978

CHAPTER 8 The Green Line

Cobban, Helena, *The Making of Modern Lebanon,* Hutchinson, 1985
The Daily Telegraph, October 1990, February 1991
The New York Times, October, November 1990
The World Almanac, Newspaper Enterprise Association Inc., New York, 1988
Newsweek, January 1991
Time Magazine, December 1990
Keesing's Contemporary Archives, Vol XXXIII, March 1987

CHAPTER 9 The Oder-Neisse Line

The European, June 1990
The Daily Express, March 1990
The Times, June, November 1990
The New York Times, July, September, November 1990
Newport (RI) Daily News, November 1990
Newsweek, December 1990
Nelson, Harold D. (ed), *Poland: A Country Study,* Washington DC, GPO for the American University, 1983.
The Treaty of Versailles, 1919

CHAPTER 10 The Wilson, The Rapallo and the Morgan Lines

Temperley, H.W.V., *A History of the Peace Conference of Paris,* Vol IV, Oxford University Press, 1921, re-printed 1969.
Cox, Geoffrey, *The Race for Trieste,* William Kimber, 1977
Herschy, Reg, *Freedom at Midnight: Austria 1938-55 A Story of the Traumatic Years of Occupation,* S.P.A. 1989
Cowgill, Brig. Anthony, Lord Brimelow, Booker, C., *The Repatriations from Austria in 1945,* Sinclair Stevenson, 1990.
The Treaty of London, 1915
The Treaty of St Germain-en-Laye, 1919
The Treaty of Rapallo, 1920
The Austrian State Treaty, 1955
Campbell, J.C., *Trieste 1954,* Princeton Univ. Press, 1976
The European, July, Sept 1991

CHAPTER 11 The 49th Parallel

National Geographic, February 1990
Morris, Richard B., *Encyclopedia of American History*, Harper and Brothers New York, 1953

CHAPTER 12 The 17th Parallel

Gima, Ronald G. (ed), *Vietnam: A Country Study*, Washington DC, GPO for the Library of Congress, 1989
The World Almanac, Newspaper Enterprise Association Inc., New York, 1988
Time Magazine, December 1990

CHAPTER 13 The 38th Parallel

Bunge, Frederica M. (ed), *North Korea: A Country Study*, Washington DC, GPO for the American University, 1981.
The New York Times, July 1990
The Daily Telegraph, September 1990

CHAPTER 14 The Radcliffe Line

Golant, William, *The Long Afternoon, British India* Hamish Hamilton, 1975.
Royle, Trevor, *The Last Days of the Raj*, Michael Joseph, 1989.
Brecher, Michael, *Nehru, A Political Biography*. Oxford University Press New York, 1959.
Tashkent Declaration, 1966.
Information Please Almanac, New York, 1979.

CHAPTER 15 The McMahon Line

The New Encyclopaedia Britannica, 1988
International Boundaries, McMahon, Journal of the Royal Soc. of Arts 84, 2, 1935
Downing, David, *An Atlas of Territorial and Border Disputes*, New English Library, 1980

Sharma, Surya Prakash, *Delimination of Land and Sea Boundaries Between Neighbouring Countries*, Lancer Books, New Delhi, 1989
Lamb, Alastair, *The McMahon Line*, Vol 2, Routledge and Kegan Paul, 1966
Woodman, Dorothy, *Himalayan Frontiers*, Barrie & Rockliff, 1969.

CHAPTER 16 The Curzon Line

Temperley, H.W.V., *A History of the Peace Conference of Paris.* Vols V, VI, Henry Frowle and Hodder and Stoughton, 1924.
The New Encyclopaedia Britannica, 1988
Fitzgerald, W., *The New Europe*, Methuen, 1946

CHAPTER 17 China-Soviet Union Frontier Disputes

Bunge, Frederica M. (ed), *China: A Country Study*, Washington DC, GPO for The American University, 1983.
Sharma, Surya Prakash, *Delimination of Land and Sea Boundaries Between Neighbouring Countries*, New Delhi, 1989.

CHAPTER 18 China-India Frontier Disputes

Bunge, Frederica M. (ed), *China: A Country Study*, Washington DC, GPO for the American University, 1983.
Downing, David, *An Atlas of Territorial and Border Disputes*, New English Library, 1980.
Woodman, Dorothy, *Himalayan Frontiers*, Barrie & Rockliff, 1969
Keegan, J. and Wheatcroft, A., *Zones of Conflict: An Atlas of Future Wars,* Cape, 1986

CHAPTER 19 Japan-Soviet Union Islands Dispute

Bunge, Frederica M. (ed), *China: A Country Study*, Washington DC, GPO for the American University, 1983.
The New York Times, October 1990
The Daily Telegraph, September 1990, February 1991, April 1992
The Japanese Peace Treaty, 1951
Rees, David, *The Soviet Seizure of the Kuriles*, Praeger, New York, 1985

CHAPTER 20 The Formosa Strait Disputed Frontier

The World Almanac, Newspaper Enterprise Association Inc., New York, 1975.
The New York Times, October 1990

CHAPTER 21 The Disputed Territory of Antarctica

National Geographic, April 1987
The Daily Telegraph, November 1990
The Times, November 1990

CHAPTER 22 Gibraltar

Hills, George, *Rock of Contention - A History of Gibraltar*, Robert Hale, 1974
Dennis, Philip, *Gibraltar*, David and Charles, 1977

CHAPTER 23 Hong Kong

Endacott, G.A., *Hong Kong Eclipse*, Oxford University Press, Hong Kong, 1978
Roberts, David, *Hong Kong*, 1990,
Gov. of Hong Kong, 1990
Fodor's Hong Kong, New York, 1989
Baedeker, *Guide to Hong Kong*, 1987
Foreign and Commonwealth Office, Private Communication, 1991

CHAPTER 24 Northern Ireland

Hickey, D.J. and Doherty, J.E., *Irish History since 1800, A Dictionary*, Gill and Macmillan, Dublin, 1980
Cook, C. and Stevenson, J., *Modern British History 1714-1987* Longman, New York, 1983
Foster, R.E. (ed), *The Oxford Illustrated History of Ireland*, Oxford Univ Press, 1989
Brady, C., O'Dowd, M. and Walker, B., *Ulster - An Illustrated History*, Batsford, 1989
Faulkner, Brian, *Memoirs of a Statesman*, Weidenfeld and Nicolson, 1978

Arnold, Bruce, *What Kind of Country - Modern Irish Politics 1968-83*, Jonathon Cape, 1984

CHAPTER 25 Africa's Disputed Frontiers

Downing, David, *An Atlas of Territorial and Border Disputes,* New English Library, 1980
Keegan, J. and Wheatcroft, A., *Zones of Conflict: An Atlas of Future Wars*, Cape, 1986
Sudan, A Country Study, Washington DC, GPO for the American University, 1983
Ethiopia, A Country Study, Washington DC, GPO for the American University, 1981
Somalia, A Country Study, Washington DC, GPO for the American University, 1982
Libya, A Country Study, Washington DC, GPO for the Library of Congress, 1989
Morocco, A Country Study, Washington DC, GPO for the Library of Congress, 1986
Kenya, A Country Study, Washington DC, GPO for the American University, 1984

CHAPTER 26 South America's Disputed Frontiers

Downing, David, *An Atlas of Territorial and Border Disputes,* New English Library, 1980
The World Almanac, Newspaper Enterprise Association Inc. New York, 1975, 1988
Bolivia, A Country Study, Washington DC, GPO for the American University, 1974
Chile, A Country Study, Washington DC, GPO for the American University, 1982
Peru, A Country Study, Washington DC, GPO for the American University, 1981
Panama, A Country Study, Washington DC, GPO for the American University, 1989
Venezuela, A Country Study, Washington DC, GPO for the American University, 1977
Ecuador, A Country Study, Washington DC, GPO for the American University, 1973

Argentina, A Country Study, Washington DC, GPO for the Library of Congress, 1986
Colombia, A Country Study, Washington DC, GPO for the Library of Congress, 1990

CHAPTER 27 Ethnic Frontiers Under Dispute

Newsweek, Nov, Dec 1990, Jan, Feb 1991, Feb 1992
The Plain Truth, Oct 1990
The New York Times, July, Oct, Nov 1990
The Times, June, Sept 1990
National Geographic, May 1987, Aug 1990, Feb 1991
The Daily Telegraph, Oct, Dec 1990, Jan, Feb, June 1991
The Sunday Times, Jan 1991
Time Magazine, Jan 1991
The European, July 1990, Jan, Aug 1991
The Sunday Express, May 1987
Temperley, H.W.V., *A History of the Peace Conference of Paris*, Vols I, IV, V, VI, Oxford University Press, 1921
Torres, John, *Belgium, Blue Guide*, Ernest Bean, 1983
Thompson, Wayne C., *The Benelux Nations*, Western Europe, Stryker-Post Pub. Washington DC, 1989.
The New Encyclopaedia Britannica, 1988
Financial Time, July 1991
Daily Mail, July 1991
The International Herald Tribune, Sept 1991
Newsweek, Feb 24, 1992

CHAPTER 28 Plebiscites As a Solution?

Wambaugh, Sarah, *Plebiscites since the World War,* Carnegie Endowment for International Peace, Washington D.C., 1933
Herschy, Reg, *Freedom at Midnight: Austria 1938-55 A story of the Traumatic Years of Occupation,* SPA, U.K., 1989

CHAPTER 29 Epilogue

The Guardian, Sept 1991
The International Herald Tribune, Aug, Sept 1991

APPENDIX

FRONTIERS DECREES, 1918, 1941.

1. THE WILSON PRINCIPLES

The Fourteen Points of 8 January 1918.

1. Open covenants of peace openly arrived at, after which there shall be no private international undertakings of any kind, but diplomacy shall proceed always frankly and in the public view.
2. Absolute freedom of navigation upon the seas outside territorial waters, alike in peace and in war, except as the seas may be closed in whole or in part by international action for the enforcement of international covenants.
3. The removal, so far as possible, of all economic barriers and the establishment of an equality of trade conditions among all the nations consenting to the peace and associating themselves for its maintenance.
4. Adequate guarantees given and taken that national armaments will be reduced to the lowest point consistent with domestic safety.
5. A free, open-minded, and absolutely impartial adjustment of all colonial claims based upon a strict observance of the principle that in determining all such questions of sovereignty the interests of the populations concerned must have equal weight with the equitable claims of the Government whose title is to be determined.
6. The evacuation of all Russian territory, and such a settlement of all questions affecting Russia as will secure the best and freest co-operation of the other nations of the world in obtaining for her an unhampered and unembarrassed opportunity for the independent determination of her own political development and national policy,

and assure her of a sincere welcome into the society of free nations under institutions of her own choosing; and more than a welcome, assistance also of every kind that she may need and may herself desire. The treatment accorded to Russia by her sister nations in the months to come will be the acid test of their goodwill, of their comprehension of her needs as distinguished from their own interests, and of their intelligent and unselfish sympathy.

7. Belgium, the whole world will agree, must be evacuated and restored without any attempt to limit the sovereignty which she enjoys in common with all other free nations. No other single act will serve as this will serve to restore confidence among the nations in the laws which they have themselves set and determined for the government of their relations with one another. Without this healing act the whole structure and validity of International Law is for ever impaired.

8. All French territory should be freed, and the invaded portions restored, and the wrong done to France by Prussia in 1871 in the matter of Alsace-Lorraine, which has unsettled the peace of the world for nearly fifty years, should be righted, in order that peace may once more be made secure in the interest of all.

9. A readjustment of the frontiers of Italy should be effected along clearly recognizable lines of nationality.

10. The peoples of Austria-Hungary, whose place among the nations we wish to see safeguarded and assured, should be accorded the freest opportunity of autonomous development.

11. Rumania, Serbia, and Montenegro should be evacuated; occupied territories restored; Serbia accorded free access to the sea; and the relations of the several Balkan States to one another determined by friendly counsel along historically established lines of allegiance and nationality; and international guarantees of the political and economic independence and territorial integrity of the several Balkan States should be entered into.

12. The Turkish portions of the present Ottoman Empire should be assured a secure sovereignty, but the other nationalities which are now under Turkish rule should be assured of an undoubted security of life and an absolutely unmolested opportunity of autonomous development, and the Dardanelles should be permanently opened as a free passage to the ships and commerce of all nations under international guarantees.

An independent Polish State should be erected which should include the territories inhabited by indisputably Polish populations, which should be assured a free and secure access to the sea, and whose political and economic independence and territorial integrity to great and small States alike.

(Wilson adds: 'An evident principle runs through the whole programme I have outlined. It is the principle of justice to all peoples and nationalities and their right to live on equal terms of liberty and safety with one another, whether they be strong or weak.')

The Four Principles of 11 February 1918.

1. That each part of the final settlement must be based upon the essential justice of that particular case and upon such adjustments as are most likely to bring a peace that will be permanent.
2. That peoples and provinces are not to be bartered about from sovereignty to sovereignty as if they were mere chattels and pawns in a game, even the great game, now for ever discredited, of the Balance of Power; but that
3. Every territorial settlement involved in this war must be made in the interest and for the benefit of the populations concerned, and not as a part of any mere adjustment or compromise of claims amongst rival States.
4. That all well-defined national aspirations shall be accorded the utmost satisfaction that can be accorded them without introducing new or perpetuating old elements of discord and antagonism that would be likely in time to break the

peace of Europe, and consequently of the world.

(It is in this speech that Wilson said: 'There shall be no annexations, no contributions, no punitive damages').

2. THE ATLANTIC CHARTER, 1941

This was a joint declaration of the United States of America and the United Kingdom, published on the 14 August 1941. It was the outcome of a meeting at sea in the early days of the month by President Roosevelt and Winston Churchill. In the following month it was approved by eight other States of the United Nations, among them the Soviet Union. Following is the text:

The President of the United States and the Prime Minister, Mr. Churchill, representing His Majesty's Government in the United Kingdom, being met together, deem it right to make known certain common principles in the national policies of their respective countries on which they base their hopes for a better future for the world.

1st, their countries seek no aggrandisement, territorial or other.

2nd, they desire to see no territorial changes that do not accord with the freely expressed wishes of the peoples concerned.

3rd, they respect the right of all peoples to choose the form of Government under which they will live; and they wish to see sovereign rights and self-government restored to those who have been forcibly deprived of them.

4th, they will endeavour, with due respect for their existing obligations, to further enjoyment by all States, great or small, victor or vanquished, of access, on equal terms to the trade and to the raw materials of the world which are needed for their economic prosperity.

5th, they desire to bring about the fullest collaboration between all nations in the economic field, with the object of securing for all improved labour standards, economic advancement and social security.

6th, after the final destruction of Nazi tyranny, they hope to see established a peace which will afford to all nations the means of dwelling in safety within their own boundaries, and which will afford assurance that all men in all the lands may live out their lives in freedom from fear and want.

7th, such a peace should enable all men to traverse the high seas and oceans without hindrance.

8th, they believe all of the nations of the world, for realistic as well as spiritual reasons, must come to the abandonment of the use of force. Since no future peace can be maintained if land sea or air armaments continue to be employed by nations which threaten, or may threaten, aggression outside of their frontiers, they believe, pending the establishment of a wider and permanent system of general security, that the disarmament of such nations is essential. They will likewise aid and encourage all other practicable measures which will lighten for peace-loving peoples the crushing burden of armament.

INDEX

AB Line	62	Antarctic, Treaty of	93, 94
Abu Dhabi	1, 5	Antofagasta	110, 111
Abu Musa	3	Antrim	100
Abyssinia	104	Antwerp	133
Acre Province		Aozou Strip	107
Act of Union (Ireland)	101	Appointed Day (Indian	
Adige River	50	Independence)	71
Adriatic	53, 54, 58, 122	Aqaba	14
Adriatic Islands	52	Arabian Sea	75
Afghanistan	79, 82	Arab states	xii
Africa	xii, 104	Arab-Israeli Conflict	13, 15
Airlift Berlin	20	Arafat, Yasir	44
Aksai Chin	87	Argentina	92, 93, 114, 115
Alaska	xiii, 60, 61	Argentina-Chile Frontier	115
Alaskan Panhandle	61, 62	Argun River	82
Al Basrah	7	Arica	110
Al Khalifa	3, 5	Arizona	60, 115
Al Qurnah	5	Armagh	100
Al Warbah, Island of	8, 9	Armenia	119, 127, 129
Albania	122, 124	Aruba, Island of	115
Alexander, Field Marshal	49, 57	Arunchal Pradesh	85
Algeria	107	Asia	xii, 110, 119
Allenstein	135	Asinello, Island of	51
Allied Kommandatura	16, 20	Assam	74
Alsace-Lorraine	158	Ataturk	11
Alto Adige	49, 50	Atlantic Charter	xiii, 48, 81, 160, 161
American War of Independence	95		
Amritsar	72	Atlee, Clement	71
Amundsen, Roald	92	Attila Line	39, 41
Amur River	82	Australia	92, 93
Anglo-Egyptian Sudan	104	Austria	20, 24, 27, 34, 37, 38, 46, 53, 80, 95, 123, 130, 133, 138
Anschluss	138		
Antarctica	xii, 92, 115	Austria-Italy frontier	35, 37, 50

Austro-Hungarian Empire	xiii, 26, 30, 34, 36, 37, 50, 117, 120, 123, 124, 132, 135, 140, 158
Austrian Habsburgs	50, 132
Austrian Netherlands	132
Austrian (Carinthian) Plebiscite (see also Carinthia)	35, 138
Austrian Silesia	30, 34
Austria-Yugoslavia frontier	38, 51, 58
Ayatollah	4
Azerbaijan	119, 127, 129
Az Zabarah	4, 5
Baghdad	11
Bahrain	1, 3, 4, 5
Balearic Islands	120
Balkans	124
Balkan States	158
Baltic States	128
Bánát	27
Bangladesh	75
Barcelona	119, 120
Barnevelt Island	115
Basque	119, 120
Basra	9
Bassas da India Island	109
Bay of Biscay	120
Bay of Valona	51
Beagle Channel	115
Beirut	xii, 14, 42, 44
Bekaa Valley	44
Bengal	71, 75
Belgium	93, 131, 132, 133, 137, 158
Belgrade	122, 124
Belize	114
Bellingshausen, F. S. von	92
Berlin	20
Berlin Airlift	20
Berlin Blockade	20
Berlin Conference (1954)	22
Berlin (East)	16, 18
Berlin (West)	16, 20
Berlin Wall	16, 18, 24, 42, 69
Bhutan	78, 82
Black Sea	xiii
Blue Line	108
Bohemia	30, 32, 33, 34
Bolivia	110
Bolzano (Bozen)	49
Bonaire Island	115
Bosgors	28
Bosnia-Herzegovina	120, 122, 125
Botswana	109
Boundary Commission Award (India)	72
Brahmaputra River	85
Bransfield, Edward	92
Bratislava	27, 32
Brazil	110
Brenner	34, 53
Brindisi	53
Britain	1, 2, 26, 91, 92, 96
British 5 Corps	56
British Eighth Army	56
British Honduras	114
British Mandate (of Iraq)	2, 6, 10
British Mandate (of Palestine)	13
British SOE Units	57
British Troops in Austria (BTA)	58
British Zone (of Carinthia)	57
Brixen	50
Brown-Palmer, Nathaniel	92
Bubiyan Island	8, 9

Bucovina	28
Budapest	28
Bulgaria	119, 122
Buraymi Oasis	5
Burgenland	26, 27
Burma	78, 82
Burundi	134
Byelorussia	129
Calcutta	71, 72
California	60, 116
Canada	xii, 9, 59, 61, 62, 131
Canidale Island	51
Canal Zone (Panama)	111
Cape Province	109
Caribbean	115
Carinthia (see also southern Carinthia)	34, 35, 36, 56, 57, 137, 139
Carinthian frontier	38
Carinthia plebiscite	35, 138
Carniola	34
Carnic Alps	50
Caspian Sea	118
Catalonia	119, 120
Castua	51
Cattaro	53
Caucasus	127
Ceausescu	29
Central African Republic	104
Central America	111, 114, 115
Ceuta	96
Chad	104, 107
Chamberlain, Neville	31
Chagos Archipelago	109
Charles, Archduke	95
Charles of Lorraine	132
Checkpoint Charlie	19
Cherso	51, 54
Chetniks	124
Chiang, Kai-Shek	91
Chile	92, 110, 111, 115
Chilwa Lake	109
China	xi, xii, 9, 64, 68, 69, 78, 82, 83, 85, 91, 98, 118, 119, 127
China-India frontier	85, 86, 87, 88
China-Soviet Union frontier (CIS)	82, 83, 84
China-Tibet frontier	84
Chindipe River	113
Chittagong Hill Tracts	72
Chobe River	109
Chou-en-Lai	86
Christian-Pagan	104
Christian Zones (Lebanon)	42
Churchill, Winston	102, 160
Cieszyn Silesia	48
Clemenceau	37
Cold War, the	22, 95
Colombia	111, 113, 115
Columbus	111
Commonwealth of Independent States (CIS)	xii, 129, 131
Communism	27, 32, 126, 127, 128
Communist Coup d'Etat	125
Communist Regime	16, 22, 23, 26, 28, 33, 63, 68
Concert of Europe	140
Confederation of Sovereign States	126
Confederation of Vienna (1815)	117, 134
Congress Party (India)	72
Convention of Peking (1860)	
Costa Rica	115

Cossacks	57	Dodecanese	35
Council of Europe	40, 130, 140	Down	100
Council of Foreign Ministers	24	Dra River	107
Court of Human Rights	140	Drau River	137
CRAMRA	94	Dravograd (Unterdrauburg)	57
Croats	52, 124, 127	Dreilander Kreuz	54
Croatia	120, 122, 123, 125	Dresden	24
Cruica Island	51	Druse	42
Crusader Interval	13	Dubai	1
CSCE	140	Dublin	102, 103
Cuba	105, 114	Dubossry	130
Cudi	12	Durand Line	79
Curacao Island	115	Durand, Sir Mortimer	79
Curzon Line	80, 81	Dushanbe	127
Curzon, Lord	80		
Cyprus	xii, 39, 40, 119		
Czechoslovakia	xiii, 27, 30, 31, 33, 48	Easter Rebellion	102
		East Germany	xiii, 16, 24
		East India Company	1
		East Pakistan	xi, 71
Dalai Lama	88	East Prussia	46
Dalmatia	35, 51, 52, 53, 54	Ecuador	113
Danube River	123	Eden, Anthony	22
Dardanelles	159	Egypt	13, 104, 107
Davis, John	92	Eire	102
Deep Bay	98	Eisach River	50
Delhi	71, 86	Elliot, Charles	99
Demilitarized Zone (DMZ)		El Arish	14
DMZ (Iraq)	10	El Salvador-Honduras	
DMZ (Korea)	66, 68, 69	frontier	114, 115
DMZ (Yugoslavia)	54	Ender, Otto	139
Desert Storm, Operation	9	Enosis	39, 40
Diego Garcia	109	EOKA	39
Dien Bien Phu	63	Eritrea	105
Dixon Entrance	62	Essequibo River	113
Djiboute	105	Estonia	128, 129
Djilas, Milovan	122, 123	ETA	119, 120
Dniester River	130	Ethiopia	104

Ethnic Frontiers	117	Gadsden Purchase	61, 116
Etorofu	89	Gadsden, James	xiii, 61
Eupen	134, 136, 137	Gagauz Turks	130
Euphrates River	5	Galilee, Sea of	3
Europa Island	109	Garden of Eden	5
European Commission	120, 128, 134	Gauntanama	114
		Gaza	13, 14
European Community	140	Geneva	41
Evout Island	115	Geneva Accord	63
		Geneva Conference	24
		Georgia	129, 130
Falkland Islands	114	German Democratic Republic (GDR)	16, 21, 23
Famagusta	41		
Feldkirch	52	German Language	51
Ferdinand, Archduke	123, 140	German Unification	46
Fermanagh	100	German-Soviet Non-agression Pact	80
Ferozepur	74		
Finland	130, 131	Germany	37, 48, 81, 128, 135
First World War	2, 10, 13, 26, 49, 123, 134, 138	Gerona	119
		Ghindipe River	113
Fiume	52, 53	Gibraltar	95, 96, 119
Flanders	xii, 131	Gila River	61
Flemish	131, 134	Gleinicke Bridge	19
Florida	60	Glorieuses Island	109
Fonesca, Gulf of	114	Goerlitz	47
Formosa	91	Golan Heights	13
Fourteen Points (of President Wilson)	31, 36, 157	Golden Temple (of Amritsar)	72
		Goli Otok	122
France	2, 9, 23, 26, 91, 92, 95, 120, 128	Gorbachev, Mikhail, President	24, 70, 84, 90, 125, 129, 130
Franco, General	119	Gorizia	35, 51, 58
Franco-Spanish Treaty (1912)	107	Gradisca	51
Frankfurt (Oder)	47	Gran Chaco	110
French Morocco	107	Grand Duchy of Warsaw	46
Frontier Treaty (Iraq-Iran, 1937)	6	Greater German Reich	37, 56
		Greater Kurdistan	10
Fruili-Venezia, Giulia	51	Greater Yugoslavia	56
		Great Lakes	59

Greece	39, 119, 122	Ho Chi Minh City	65
Greek Cypriots	39	Hokkaido	89
Greek Cypriot Zone	39, 41	Holland	133
Green Line, Beirut	42, 44	Home, Lord	102
Green Line, Cyprus	xii, 41	Honecker, Erich	19
Grosse Schutte	27	Honduras	115
Gruica Island	51	Hong Kong	xiii, 98
Guantanama	114	Hormuz, Strait of	5
Guatemala	114	Huancabamba	113
Guatemala-Honduras Frontier	114, 115	Hughes Bay	92
		Hungary	24, 26, 27, 28, 122, 130, 135
Guayaquil Treaty (1829)	113		
Guir River	107	Hussein, Saddam	7
Gujarat	75		
Gulf	xi, 1		
Gulf Cooperation Council (GCC)	5	Idria Pass	51
Gulf Islands	3	Ilemi Triangle	108
Gulf War	10, 12, 15	Incan Empire	110
Guyana	113	India	xi, 71, 72, 74, 82, 85
Gurdesdur	72	Indian-Afghanistan Frontier	79
Gypsies	130	Indian Massacres	74
		Indian Ocean Islands Disputes	109
		Indochina	63
Habomai Island Group	89	Inner Mongolia	82, 84, 127
Habsburg Empire	31	IRA (Irish Republican Army)	100, 102, 119
Halabjah	12		
Hanoi	63	Iran-Iraq War	5, 9
Hawar Islands	4	Iran	3, 4, 7, 8, 11, 119
Heilongjiang Province	82	Iraq	2, 3, 4, 6, 7, 8, 9, 10, 11, 13, 119
Henry II	101		
Herschel	109	Iraq-Iran Frontier	6
Hillsborough Agreement	103	Iraq (Treaty of)	9, 10
Himalayan frontier	xii	Ireland	101, 102
Himalayas	78, 185	Irish Free State	100
Hindus	72, 73, 74	Iron Curtain	19, 130
Hitler, Adolf	28, 31, 37, 138	Islam	123, 127
Hitler-Stalin Pact	128	Isonzo River	58
Ho Chi Minh	63	Israel	xii, 13, 14, 42

Istria	35, 51, 54
Italian Frontier	38
Italy	26, 35, 36, 37, 105
Italy-Austria Frontier	35, 37, 38, 49
Italy-Yugoslavia Frontier	38, 49, 50, 52, 54, 58
Jammu	75
Japan	xii, 63, 89, 90, 99
Japan-Soviet Union Islands' Dispute	89
Jinnah, Mohammed Ali	72
Jordan	13
Jordan River	13
Juan de Fuca Strait	60
Juan de Nova Island	109
Julian Alps	51
Kagera	108
Kanaltal	37, 52
Kansas	116
Karachi	71
Karakoram Mountain	87
Karawanken Alps	52, 57
Karelia (Finland)	131
Kashmir	xi, 73, 74, 75, 88
Kassala-Gallabat	105
Kazakhstan	84, 129
Kazungula	109
Kennedy, John F., President	24
Kenneret Lake	3
Kenya	105, 108
Khanaqin	11
Khawr al Udayd	5
Khrushchev Nikita	23, 24
Khrushchev Ultimatum	24
Kim Il Sung, President	70
Kirghizia	84, 127, 128, 129
Kirkuk	9, 10, 12
Klagenfurt	36, 56, 57
Klagenfurt Basin	52
Klondike	61
Kongka Pass	87
Korea-North and South (see also Democratic People's Republic and Republic of Korea)	66, 67, 68, 69
Korean War	66, 69
Kosovo	122, 124, 125
Kostrzyn	48
Kowloon	98
Krain	34
Kremlin	129
Kublai Khan	63
Kunashiri	89
Kuointang (Guomindang)	91
Kurd enclaves	11
Kurdish Democratic Party (KDP)	12
Kurdish Workers Party (PKK)	12
Kurdistan	10, 11
Kurds	xii, 10, 11, 12
Kurile Islands	89, 90
Kuwait	1, 3, 5, 7, 8, 9
Kyrenia	41
Ladakh	85
Ladins	50
Lagosta	53, 54
Lahore	71, 72
Lake of the Woods	59
La Linea	97
Laos	82
Latvia	128, 129
Lausanne, Treaty of (1919)	2, 9

League of Nations	10, 134	Malmedy	134, 136, 137
Lebanon	2, 13, 42, 44	Mandate, Class A	6
Leipzig	24	Mangart, Mount	51
Lefta	41	Maramom River	113
Leningrad	128	Marburg (Maribor)	57
Lennox Island	115	Maria Theresa	132
Lesotho	109	Marienwerde	135
Lerida	119	Maromite Militia	42
Leticia Corridor	113	Massachusetts	59
Libya	107	Masuria	46
Lissa	53	Matatiele	109
Litani River	3	Matsu	91
Lithuania	120, 128, 129	Mattuglia	51
Lloyd George	26, 37	Mauretania	108
London Agreement (1831)	133	Mauritius	109
London Treaty (1915)	49	Melilla	96
Londonderry	100	Mesilla Valley	61
Louisiana Purchase	59	Mexico	xiii, 60, 61, 116, 120
Lower Austria	30	Meskhetian Turks	127
Lussin	51, 54	Mesopotamia	11
Luxembourg	93	Middle East Frontiers	1
Lvov	48	Mississippi River	60
		Moldavia	129, 130
		Moliro	109
MacArthur, General	68	Monfalcone	58
MacMillan, Harold	56	Mongolia	82, 84
McMahon Line	78, 85, 86	Montenegro	122, 125, 158
McMahon, Sir Henry	78, 85	Moravia	30, 33, 34
Macedonia	120, 122, 125	Morgan, General	49
Madrid	120	Morgan Line	38, 49, 58
Magellan Strait	114	Morocco	107
Magyar Hirlap	28	Moscow	84, 127, 130
Magyar Irredenta	26	Moslems	42, 44, 71, 72, 74, 84, 119, 125, 127
Maine	59		
Makarios, Archbishop	39, 40	Moslem Zones (Lebanon)	42
Malagasy Republic	109	Mosul	9, 10, 136
Malawi	108, 109	Mozambique	109
Malawi, Lake	108	Mountbatten, Lord	71, 72, 74

Munich	31	Nueva Island	115
Munoz Vernaza			
Suarez Treaty (1916)	113		
Musandam Peninsula	5	Oder-Neisse Line	24, 46, 47, 48
Muslim League Party	72	Oder River	46
Mussolini	37	Oetz	50
		Ogaden	105
		Okinawa	90
Namibia	109	Oklahoma	116
Napoleon	60, 133	Oman	1, 2, 3, 5
Napo-Putamayo River	113	Operation Desert Storm	9
Nazis	26, 32, 48, 56, 128, 160	Opium Wars	98
Natal	109	Orange Free State	109
NATO	95, 134, 140	Oregon	59
Nazism	27	Osh	127
Nei Monggol	82	Ottoman	9, 119
Neisse River	46, 47	Ottoman Empire	2, 7, 10, 13, 26, 39, 117, 124, 159
Nepal	82		
Nehru, Pandit	72	Ouaddai	104
Netherlands	94	Oxford	71
Nevada	60, 116		
New Brunswick	59		
New Delhi	86, 88	Pacific	xii
New Mexico	60, 116	Pacific Ocean	110
New Territories	98	Pacific War (1879-84)	89, 110
New York	59, 128	Pakistan	xi, 71, 73
New Zealand	92, 93	Pakistan, East	71, 74, 75
Nicaragua	114, 115	Pakistan, West	71
Nicaragua-Costa		Palazzuoli Island	51
Rica Frontier	114, 115	Palestine	2, 3, 13
Nicaragua-Honduras Frontier	114	Palestine Liberation	
Nicosia	41	Organisation (PLO)	14, 44
Nixon, Richard, President	65	Palestinians	42
Nogorna-Karabakh	119, 127	Palmer, Nathaniel Brow	92
North Korea, see Korea		Palmerston, Lord	99
North Vietnam	xii, 63, 65	Pamir	82
Northern Ireland	100	Panama	111, 112
Norway	92	Panmunjom	68, 69, 70

Paraguay	110	Plebiscite, Cyprus	39
Parallel (Latitude)		Plebiscite, Sopron	27
36 degrees	12	Plebiscites	xiii, 3, 27, 34, 53, 134,
49 degrees	59	Plebiscites cont'd.	135
17 degrees	63	Podbendo Pass	51
38 degrees	66	Podlanisam Pass	51
Para River	87	Poland	xiii, 24, 46, 48, 80, 130,
Paris	34, 72		159
Paris Peace		Polisaria	108
Conference (1919-1923)	xi, 1,	Pomerania	46, 48
	80, 120 135	Pope, The	101
Paris Peace Treaties: see Peace		Potsdam	19
Treaties of Paris		Potsdam Conference	20, 23
Park Chung Hee, President	69	Portugal	3
Peace Treaties of Paris	xiii, 49, 117,	Prague	32
	120	Predil Pass	51
Pec	54	Prince Albert	99
Pedemonte-Mosquera		Prince Bishop of Trent	50
Protocol (1830)	113	Prince William of Orange	133
Peking	84, 90, 98	Princip, Geyrilo	123
Pelagosa	53, 54	Protection Powers (Berlin)	21
Peoples Liberation Front (PLF)	105	Prussia	30, 46, 48, 158
Democratic Peoples Republic		Pula (Pola)	52, 53, 58
of Korea	66	Punjab	71, 72, 73, 74
Peoples Revolutionary Democratic		Putamayo River	113
Front (PRDF)	105	Pyrenees	120
Perestroika	125		
Persian Gulf States	1		
Peru	110, 113	Qatar	1, 3, 4, 5
Pescadores (Penghus)	91	Quebec	62
Pesh Merga	12	Queen Victoria	99
Pesti Hirlap	28	Quemoy	91
Petrograd	128		
Phelange	42		
Phillip V	95	Radcliffe Line	71, 73, 74
Picton	115	Radcliffe, Sir Cyril	71, 72, 73
Piz Umbrail	50	Rafah	14
Plavnik Unie Island	51	Rapallo Line	38, 49, 54, 58

171

Rapallo, Treaty of (1920)	38, 49, 54
Ram of Cutch	74
Ras al Khaymah	4
Ras Muhammed	14
Ravi River	72
Reagan, Ronald, President	19
Red Line	41, 108
Red Sea	14
Reichstag	21
Renner, Karl, President	34, 138
Republic of Ireland	102
Republic of Korea	66
Republic of Vietnam	63
Reschen	50
Reuter, Ernst	21
Rhetian Alps	50
Riga	128
Rijeka (Fiume)	52
Rio Grande	60
Rocky Mountains	59
Roh Tae Woo, President	70
Romania (Rumania)	26, 27, 130, 158
Rome	51
Ronse	134
Rooke, Sir George	95
Roosevelt, President	160
Royal Engineers	72
Russia	26, 46, 82, 98, 126, 129, 157, 158
Russian-Polish War	80
Rwanda	134
Saar	136
Saddam Hussein	7
Saharan Arab Democratic Republic (SADR)	108
Sahin Line	41
Saigon	63
Saint Vith	134
Sakhalin	90
Salzburg	136, 139
Sampson, Nikes	40
San Francisco	90
San Pietro di Nembi Island	51
Sanssouci Palace	20
Sarajevo	140
Sardinia	51
Saudi Arabia	3, 5, 7, 8, 13
Save (Sava) River	51, 123
Scheldt	133
Schneeberg	51
Scotland	xii
Scottish National Party	xii
Scott, Lady	94
Scott, Robert Falcon	92
Scott, Sir Peter	94
Schleswig	136
Schonburgh Line	113
Sebenico	53
Second New Zealand Division	56
Second World War	xiii, 28, 32, 35, 38, 46, 47, 49, 56, 63, 89, 90, 117, 120, 122, 124, 130
Senkaku	90
Seoul	69, 70
Serbia	52, 120, 122, 124, 125, 158
Serb-Croat-Slovene State (Kingdom of)	52, 123
Sevan, Robert	94
Sèvres, Treaty of (1920)	2, 10
Sexten Valley	52, 54
Shackleton, Sir Ernest	92
Shah of Iran	3, 6
Sharjah	1, 4
Sha Tau Kok	98

Shatt al Arab Waterway	5, 6	Soviet Empire	xii
Shevardnadze, Eduard	84	Soviet Military Commandant	
Shiite Militia	42	(of Berlin)	22
Shikotan	89	Soviet-Polish Border	80
Shum Chan River	98	Soviet Union	xii, 9, 11, 19, 21, 23,
Siberia	118	28, 46, 48, 56, 57, 64, 68, 69, 81, 82,	
Sicily	51	83, 84, 85, 90, 119, 125, 126, 127,	
Sikhs	72, 73, 74	130, 131, 140, 160	
Sikkin	82	Soviet Zone (of Germany)	20, 21
Silesia	30, 46, 48, 136	Spain	95, 96, 97, 108, 110, 111,
Simla	78		119, 120
Sinkiang	87	Spanish Morocco	107
Sino-British Treaty	99	Spanish Sahara	108
Sino-Indian Boundary	86	Spanish South America	110
Sino-Indian War	78	Stalin	22, 128
Sinai	13, 14	Stelvia	50
Six Day War	14	St. Germain-en-Laye,	
Skopje	122	Treaty of (1919)	27, 34, 35
Slavs	53	Stone Cutters Island	98
Slovakia	30, 33	St. Petersburg	128
Slovene Carinthia	56	Strait of Hormuz	5
Slovene Carinthian Partisans	56	St. Veit	52
Slovenes	34, 35, 52, 138	Styria	34, 56
Slovenia	34, 36, 57, 120, 125	Subotica	123
Slubice	47, 48	Sudan	104, 105, 108
SOE	57	Sudetenland	31, 34
Somalia	105	Suez	14
Sopron	27, 135	Sundarong Chin Valley	85
South Africa	93, 94, 109	Sykes-Picot Agreement	2, 3
South America	xii, 110, 120, 131	Sylhet	72
Southern Lebanon	44	Syria	2, 11, 13, 44, 119
Southern Carinthia	xiii, 34, 56,	Syrian-Iraq Frontier	2
	135, 137	Switzerland	139
South Ossetian	130		
South Tirol	xiii, 34, 35, 36, 37, 38,		
	49, 51, 135	Tacna	111
South Vietnam	xii, 63, 65	Tadzhikistan	84, 127
Soviet Communist Party	126	Taipei	90

Taiwan	90, 91
Tallinn	128
Tanzania	108
Tarragona	119
Tarrenz	138
Tarvis (Tarvisio)	52, 54, 56
Tarvis, Mount	50
Tashkent	75
Tegel Airport	20
Tempelhof Airport	21
Texas	116
Thalweg	7
Thatcher, Margaret	94
Tibet	78, 84, 85, 86, 87, 127
Tierra del Fuego	115
Tigris River	5
Tirgu Mures	28
Tirol	50, 51, 139
Tito	56, 57, 58, 120, 122
Toblach, Mount	50
Tongeren	134
Toshiki Kaifu (Prime Minister of Japan)	90
Traiskirchen	130
Transkei	109
Transylvania	26, 28, 29, 36
Treaty of Ghent (1814)	59
Treaty of Peace (1947) Italy	58
Treaty of Lausanne (1919)	119
Treaty of London (1839)	133, 134
Treaty of London (1915)	35, 36, 37, 49, 50, 54
Treaty of London Line	38, 49, 52, 53, 54
Treaty of Nanking (1842)	98
Treaty of Rapallo (1920)	38, 49, 54
Treaty of St. Germain (1919)	27, 34, 35, 54, 139
Treaty of The Final Settlement (German Unification)	25
Treaty of Trianon	26, 27, 28
Treaty of Utrecht (1713)	95, 96
Treaty of Versailles (1783)	95
Treaty of Versailles (1919)	30, 46
Trent (Trient, Trentino)	49, 50, 51
Tricorno (Terglu)	51
Trieste	35, 51, 52, 56, 57, 58
Trinity Island	92
Trinquet Line	107
Tripoli	44
Troemlin Island	109
Truman, Harry, President	68
Turbs	3
Turkey	6, 9, 10, 11, 12, 39, 117, 119, 130, 159
Turkestan	117
Turkish Cypriot Zone	39, 41
Turkmenistan	127, 129
Two Plus Four (Treaty)	25
Tyrone	100
Uganda	108
Ukraine	128, 129
Ulster	102, 103
Umm al Aysh	8
Umm Qasr	8
United Arab Emirates (UAE)	1, 3, 5
United Kingdom	23, 71, 80, 93, 97, 101, 160
United Kingdom of the Netherlands	133
United Nations	3, 9, 40, 58, 68, 70, 91, 96, 97, 128, 140, 141
United States	9, 15, 19, 23, 37, 59, 62, 65, 68, 80, 90, 94, 101, 120, 160

United States-Canada frontier	xii, 59	Vistgau (Val Venosta)	50
United States-Mexico Border	60	Volosca	51
Unterdrauburg (Dravograd)	57	Vojvodina	122
Upper Jordan River	3	Vorarlberg	136, 139
Upper Silesea, see Silesia		Vukovar	123
Uqair, (Treaty of)	8		
USS Pueblo	69		
Ussuri River	82	Wallonia	xii, 131
Ustashi	124	Walloons	134
Utah	60, 116	Waremme	134
Uzbekistan	127, 129	Waterloo	134
Uzbek Turks	119	War of Spanish Succession (1720)	95
		Weizsacher, Richard von	19
Val Canale	37, 52	West Bank	13, 14
Val d'Aosta	51	West Berlin	16
Valencia (see also Bay of)	120	Western European Union	140
Valona	53	Western Giulia	58
Val Venosta, see Vistgau		Western Hungary	27
Vancouver Island	60	Western Occupation Powers	21, 22
Vatra Romaneasea	28	Western Romania	29
Venice	53	West Germany	20
Venezia Giulia	52, 56, 57, 58	Wilson Line	38, 49, 53
Venezuela	113, 115	West Pakistan	xi
Vermont	59	Wilson Principles	31, 34, 36, 157, 158, 159
Versailles, Treaties of	26		
Victoria	99	Wilson, Woodrow, President	31, 49, 52, 53
Vienna	20, 52, 130		
Vienna Decision (1940)	28	Wyoming	116
Vietnam (Democratic Republic of) see also North and South Vietnam	63, 82	Xinjiang	84
Villach	37, 52, 57		
Villach-Faak Road	36		
Villach-Feldkirch-St.Veit Railway	52	Yalta	46, 80
Vilna	48, 128, 136	Yarmuk River	3
Vilnius, see Vilna		Yasir Arafat	44
Vina del Mar	94	Yeltsin, Boris	125, 126

Yom Kippur	14
Ypres	134
Yugoslav Federation	xii, 120
Yugoslav Frontier	52, 56
Yugoslav Partisans	56
Yugoslav-Austria Frontier	51
Yugoslavia	xii, 27, 34, 53, 54, 56, 58, 120, 122, 123, 124, 137, 139, 140, 141
Yukon	61

Zagreb	123
Zaire	109
Zakhu	12
Zambesi River	109
Zambia	109
Zemun	122
Zgorzelec	47
Ziller	50
Zimbabwe	109
Zira	74
Zone A (Trieste)	58
Zone B (Yugoslav controlled)	58